LIFE IS BLACK AND WHITE

TONY WALSTER

BALBOA
PRESS

A DIVISION OF HAY HOUSE

Balboa Press books may be ordered through booksellers or by contacting:

Balboa Press
A Division of Hay House
1663 Liberty Drive
Bloomington, IN 47403
www.balboapress.co.uk
1 (877) 407-4847

Because of the dynamic nature of the Internet, any web addresses or links contained in this book may have changed since publication and may no longer be valid. The views expressed in this work are solely those of the author and do not necessarily reflect the views of the publisher, and the publisher hereby disclaims any responsibility for them.

The author of this book does not dispense medical advice or prescribe the use of any technique as a form of treatment for physical, emotional, or medical problems without the advice of a physician, either directly or indirectly. The intent of the author is only to offer information of a general nature to help you in your quest for emotional and spiritual well-being. In the event you use any of the information in this book for yourself, which is your constitutional right, the author and the publisher assume no responsibility for your actions.

Print information available on the last page.

ISBN: 978-1-9822-8024-6 (sc)
ISBN: 978-1-9822-8023-9 (e)

Balboa Press rev. date: 10/15/2018

Dedication

I would like to thank my wife Angie for supporting me whilst I have been writing my book, my family and friends that have help me with gathering the information and my Mother in Law Anne for finding it interesting.

L ife is very complex and intricate every decision we make is made for a reason either consciously or more often than not sub consciously. Your choice of school friends, your hobbies, your career pathway, your car (not just because it is the cheapest) your life partner or partners, the foods you like and don't like your tastes in music. These are decisions we have all made throughout our life, some we have been helped with others we have made alone. Many people like sport, a majority of them are football supporters! They choose their team in many different ways guided by their family or friends, (I told my two children there are 92 teams in England support any one of 91 of them if you support the 92nd "out you go") swayed by the media, (more so these days) the team your friends follow and obviously the local team to where you live that is usually the team you follow. When I decided that football would be my sport of choice I had no family to guide me (no one was interested in football) no local league team for the majority of my childhood. Birmingham was over 20 miles from Colwall and Reading over 20 miles away from Newbury and for the year I was in Nottingham there were two teams to worry about and so I had 92 League teams to choose from! Which one should I choose and why? Because the one thing I realised even at a young age is the team you choose is your team for life! Unless you are a "Glory Hunter" which certainly happened with some people I knew and went to school with in Nottingham who were supporters of many different teams when I moved away from Nottingham in the mid-70s but when I came back to Nottingham in the early 80s they were all "loyal" Forest supporters!

I was born, the youngest of 3 children, and brought up on a small farm in a tiny village with a population of less than 1000 by the name of

Colwall nestling at the foot of the Malvern Hills in Worcestershire on the Herefordshire side of the hills approximately five miles from Malvern, fifteen miles from Hereford and ninety three miles from Meadow Lane so why am I a Notts County fan? My Mum, Dad and both my elder sisters were born in Nottingham but the family had moved to Colwall before I entered the world. My Dad was the oldest of 4, my Mum the oldest of 5 none of whom showed the slightest interest in football but my Dad's father, my Grandad was a "dyed in the wool" Nottingham Forest fan as I was told on the few occasions that we visited Epperstone in Nottingham to the farm where they lived or when they visited us throughout my formative years. Usually we visited Nottingham just once a year near Christmas and they visited us in the summer and on these visits I was constantly regaled with stories of trips to away grounds such as Hillsborough, Highbury, Elland Road and Anfield, most of which at that time I had never even heard of, as well as matches at the City Ground he had attended over the years and always with the promise to take me to the City Ground one day but more often than not the story was of of their FA Cup win in 1959 at Wembley 2:1 against Luton Town which he had attended. At 4 and 5 the stories were great to listen to but honestly did not mean that much to me, as I had never even seen a football match of any sort by then.

It was an idyllic childhood the fields on the farm were my playground and during the holidays especially in the summer I was rarely at home from dawn to dusk getting in the way as the harvest was gathered in and roaming the fields and adjacent woodland this fun was only interrupted by school, sadly, which was about a mile away and rain or shine Winter or Summer us children walked there and back me in shorts. At about 5 years old I drove my first tractor over my bicycle and through a fence, which it has to be said did not impress anybody. The first football match I vaguely remember seeing was the FA Cup final of 1969/70 because of the names of some of the players Bonetti, Harris, Osgood, Bremner, Lorimer and Clarke and because the boys who were that bit older at school were Leeds United supporters. (wherever Leeds was?) So I guess I was? I knew no better! There was no school football team just a "kick around" in the playground at lunchtimes, although not every lunchtime, games like "British Bulldog" and Tunnel Tag proving far more popular! Well it was only a small village! so the only time I ever got near a football pitch was when the Colwall Scout Group founded in 1967 played games and it soon became very apparent that I was not much of a footballer! I started at Left Back then was switched to Right Back! Right Back in the changing rooms! I did become very adept at carrying a tray of oranges out onto the pitch at half time so I did have a use.

In early 1972 that was all to change for me and many others in the village. Hereford United had got through to the 3rd Round of the FA Cup and a tie with League One giants Newcastle United at St James' Park. The local press was full of it and most people were talking about it. As a Non League club albeit a good one Hereford entered the FA Cup in the 4th Qualifying Round in November 1971 with a home game against fellow Non League side and local rivals Cheltenham Town on Saturday November 6th 1971 winning 3:0. Their reward in the 1st round proper was an Away game at fellow Non League side King's Lynn on Saturday November 20th 1971 where they got a 0:0 draw winning the replay at home on Wednesday 24th 1:0. There was no waiting 10 days to play a replay in those days. Round 2 was a game at home to League 4 side Northampton Town on Saturday December 11th which finished 0:0, the replay at Northampton on Tuesday 14th finished 2:2. The 3rd game, they played more than one replay in those days, was played at a neutral venue at West Bromwich Albion on Monday December 20th and Hereford won 2:1 after extra time so got to the 3rd Round and a game at Newcastle on January 15th 1972 sadly postponed not once but twice due to a waterlogged pitch. The game was eventually played on Monday 24th January by which time both teams knew the winner would be at home to West Ham in the 4th Round and Hereford came away with a fabulous 2:2 draw thanks to a late equaliser and so to a replay which was again postponed three times for waterlogging before being played on 4th round day Saturday 5th February 1972 at Edgar Street then the local hysteria started front to back local paper coverage and the first question anyone you saw asked you was about Hereford. Amazingly Hereford won the replay 2:1 after extra time, Ronnie Radford scoring to equalise a first goal by Malcolm McDonald, then Ricky George getting the winner. West Ham thus visited on Wednesday February 9th and drew 0:0, the replay being played at Upton Park on Monday February 14th with a 2:15pm kick off due to the three day week and power shortages. A Geoff Hurst hat trick saw

West Ham through 3:1. Even after such an amazing FA Cup run Hereford had enough in them to finish Runners up in the Southern League at the end of the season and were consequently elected to the Football League at the expense of Barrow. My first real live game memory was the 1972/73 Cup Final (as I had Chicken Pox at the time and Mum and Dad had gone away for the weekend to Bruges in Belgium on a holiday they had won). Again Leeds were involved and again they were beaten, this time by Sunderland, in one of the major shocks of all time. I sat and watched the whole game and slowly without realising it I was developing the "bug" for football.

On Friday 12th April 1974 we moved from Colwall to an even smaller village called Bothampstead seven miles North of Newbury in Berkshire and one hundred and thirty three miles from Meadow Lane. Even worse, it consisted quite literally of a few houses and a pub, no shops and nothing else and a much larger farm where my dad worked. The main part of the farm and the dairy was about a mile down the road and it was my job to cycle every day with a small milk churn to fetch the milk fresh from the cows. It was more than 2 miles along the B4009, a very busy road that ran from the centre of Newbury to Tring, to school every morning. I went by bicycle every day but at least I was allowed to wear long trousers in the winter. Talk of football at school such as it was at that time was still all about such teams as Leeds United and Chelsea little mention of the local team Reading and strangely no mention at all of Hereford and again there was no school football team and very little football played in the playground. My grand parents visited us at the beginning of May 1974 in the week leading up to the FA Cup final, Liverpool V Newcastle United. I felt really grown up as a 9 year old shaking my Grandad's hand as he walked into the house. Once they had settled down he asked me who I wanted to win the Cup. In all innocence I said Newcastle, that did not go down at all well and it was only years later I found out the real reason Nottingham Forest had played Newcastle in an earlier round (the Quarter Finals) at St James Park and early in the second half Forest were awarded a penalty and went 3:1 up, Newcastle also had a player sent off. The home fans invaded the pitch and two Forest players were injured in the skirmish that ensued. Once order was restored the referee having consulted both managers continued the game Newcastle finally winning 4:3. The FA ordered a replay at Goodison Park, which finished

0:0 after extra time so a second replay was needed also at Goodison Park, which Newcastle won 1:0. To this day many older Forest supporters feel cheated. When it came to the World Cup final of 1974 Holland were the choice of the few children, who knew anything about football, including me? Krol, Rep, Rensenbrink, Neeskens and of course Cruyff the names still so familiar so many years later what a team. Holland got to the final where they met West Germany and scored a penalty in the 2nd minute but by half time they were 2:1 down and that was how it finished. To this day many pundits believe that that Holland side was the best team never to win the World Cup. Sadly I couldn't watch the final as I was at an air show at Greenham Common but I do remember Scotland being the first country ever to be knocked out a World Cup Finals without losing a game. They comfortably beat Zaire but only 2:0 and the lack of goals was the reason they came home early. They drew with Brazil 0:0 so needed to beat Yugoslavia in their last game to be sure to progress. They drew 1:1 and Brazil beat Zaire 3:0! at one stage Brazil won a free kick and the Zaire player Mwepu Ilunga ran from the wall and kicked the ball and got sent off! And Scotland came home.

We only stayed in Bothampstead for just under a year and then on Thursday 27th March 1975 we moved again, this time to Gedling in Nottingham to a house on Brooklands Drive across the main Burton Road from the Inn for a Penny public house, where I was enrolled at All Hallows Junior School in Mrs Blaine's class again walking to and from school every day. I played football in the playground and occasionally on the football pitch next to the school but this wasn't exactly the flattest piece of ground in Nottingham so I still had little chance to improve my "footballing skills" but because of my skills for serving half time oranges I was chosen to accompany the school first team when they played local rivals Priory School before the Summer Holidays. (I think we won but it was a long time ago and I cannot honestly remember) but what an honour. I joined the First Gedling Cubs and was involved in two matches playing for them in the first match and as the opponents only had 10 players in the second match having the ignominy of being "loaned" to them for the second game, I was that good. I got to know more about the two local football teams than my Grandad had ever told me from the other children such as Notts being known as County despite playing within the City Boundary and that on no account should Forest be known as Notts Forest. Finally the chance arose for my Grandad to keep his promise and so on Saturday 12th April 1975 I found myself sitting in the Main Stand at the City Ground with a red and white scarf round my neck (he had given me the one he had worn at Wembley in 1959 and I have to admit I still have that scarf ..... somewhere!) watching Forest who were 17th in the league play Southampton who were 12th in League Division 2 in front of a crowd of 11554 it finished 0:0. I have no idea how much it cost to get in as my Grandad paid? I honestly cannot remember much about that day apart from the fact I had never been anywhere with that many other people in such a confined space before in my life, making it feel both scary but exhilarating and the fact he bought me a packet of Extra Strong Mints. If that was a live football match I was not impressed no thanks, I'll pass. At the time of the match my Grandad was 74 and promised me, if I wanted to, he would take me once or twice the following season.

In the meantime where my Dad was working, there was a Notts County supporter, Len Wright who along with his son Mark visited Meadow Lane every other week as well as going to some away games. He said he was more than happy to take me anytime the following season if I wanted. So on the 23rd of August 1975, Notts County played their first home game of the season having already picked up three points out of four in their first two away games of the season. They won 2:1 at the Valley against Charlton with Eric Probert scoring the winner, after Les Bradd had equalised and drawing 1:1 at Brisbane Road against Orient with Eric Probert putting Notts in front early on and standing third in the fledgling league. That was my first ever visit to Meadow Lane. It cost me 30 pence to get in (which was a whole weeks pocket money) to watch Notts County play Southampton who were 9th in League Division Two. Yes Southampton again and amazingly the same score 0:0, this time with a crowd of 9439. I stood behind the dug outs in front of the main stand. The ground as we all remember was never going to be spectacular, I would describe it as homely. The scoreboard fascinated me and at times held my attention more than the game. I remember little else about that first game apart from seeing Jimmy Sirrel in the dugout, hearing him shout and not understanding a word but it felt right, it felt good and I wanted to go again if I could. The following week as it was still the school summer holidays there was an Open Day at the City Ground. I remember going walking around and even walking on the pitch thinking there were 6 goals and I wondered which net they had been scored in. Forest had beaten Rotherham 5:1 in the second leg of the First Round of the League Cup that week. Despite many hours spent in the archive section of Nottingham Library I can find no information about this but I am positive I didn't dream it. That weekend Saturday August 30th Notts were away at the City Ground, sadly my Grandad couldn't take me and I wasn't allowed to go with Len because of the possibility of crowd trouble. That was the reason I was given by my parents so I had to make do with watching Les Bradd score a 90th minute winner on Star Soccer on the Sunday afternoon but at least I could spend my pocket money on sweets. The following Saturday Carlisle were duly dispatched 1:0 with an Eric Probert goal and then another first Sunderland at home in the League Cup on Tuesday 9th September 1975. My first ever game under floodlights. Silly things you remember on the way into the ground, a car was on fire on Meadow Lane and as the night drew in and the floodlights got brighter, the people in the County Road stand opposite to me flicking their cigarette lighters on and off every now and then, another win 2:1 with goals by Brian Stubbs to equalise before half time and then a late winner from Les Bradd making it another very satisfactory night. Before the next home league game the draw for the third round of the League Cup was made. The Mighty Leeds United Away at Elland Road oh boy! Less than a fortnight later the day after I turned 11, Luton Town were duly beaten at home 1:0 with an Ian Scanlon goal. Again I remember very little apart from the fact Eric Morecambe was sat just behind me in the Main Stand, pipe in mouth, watching the game. By now Notts were sending tickets to school so I was able to use my pocket money for sweets and comics. By the time the Leeds game came around on Wednesday October 8th 1975 Notts had lost the one game all season, a 4:0 hammering at Roker Park Sunderland at the end of September, and hopes were high for the team and for my chances of going with Len and Mark. Sadly I was not allowed to for the same reason again, the chance of trouble and because it was a midweek game, so I had to make do with listening to Radio 2. Exciting but by no means a substitute for the real thing (I have still never been to Elland Road all these years later). Back then First Division Clubs didn't rest their top players for cup games against lower league opposition as they do now and still Notts won 1:0 with an Ian Scanlon goal in the second half and then drew Everton away in the fourth round, another First Division Club, on their own ground. Maybe I could go this time? Between the cup rounds there was a major shock as Jimmy Sirrel left to become manager of Sheffield United, and his Assistant Ron Fenton took over as manager at Notts. How much of a shock I don't think anybody realised at the time certainly not 11 year old me. The season was progressing nicely by the time of the Everton game and again hopes were high and again I wasn't allowed to go. Not fair, Radio 2 for me once more and another great result on Tuesday November 11th a 2:2 draw with goals from Ian Scanlon and Brian Stubbs to twice equalise goals from Gary Jones and David Irving and a replay at Meadow Lane (again I have still never been to Goodison Park). As the season was still progressing nicely the Everton replay could not come round quickly enough and when the match was finished on Tuesday November 25th 1975 Notts had won 2:0 with both goals from Les Bradd in front of 23404 supporters. The big thing I remember about the game was Bob Latchford the Everton striker standing in one of the turnstile boxes near the Chestnut Tree at the end of the Main Stand signing autographs. One of which adorns my autograph book. Wherever is it all these years later. Another fabulous result and an even better draw in the fifth round the Mighty Newcastle United at St James Park! As Hereford had beaten them in 1972 why couldn't Notts three years later? I didn't even bother asking to go this time, I knew what the answer would be so yet again I settled down listening to Radio 2 on Wednesday December 5th 1975. I am sure every Notts fan irrespective of age and whether they were present or not remembers what happened that night? Malcolm MacDonald took one of his famous long throw ins with the wind behind him and Notts goalkeeper Eric McManus going up to catch it under no pressure managed to drop the ball over the line! And our cup run was over. (Newcastle got to the final losing 2:1 to Manchester City)! Suffice to say, at 11 it was not very painful, more comical, but as I grew up I realised how much of a mistake it was. Christmas was fast approaching and the draw for the 3rd round of the FA Cup was made, Leeds United again, this time at home. I was so excited, the last League game before the Leeds game was on December 27th 1975 at home to Oldham Athletic resulting in a 5:1 win with 2 goals from both Les Bradd and Ian Scanlon and the other from John Sims to warm us all up. As usual I was standing behind the dug outs and at half time two supporters behind me who had certainly had a shandy or three were singing "going up going up going up" tonelessly but to my great confusion. Who was going up where and why? Before kick off after the Boxing Day game against Fulham at Craven Cottage which Notts lost 3:2 Mick Vinter and Ian Scanlon scoring after Notts had been two down but Fulham getting an 88th minute winner Notts stood 5th in the league on 29 points 3 points off promotion and 5 points above Forest! We were to finish the season 5th but 4 points off promotion and 3 points above Forest! Promotion and relegation were totally unknown to me at the time. Blimey over the last 40 years as a Notts fan I have got to know both outcomes on a fairly regular basis. The New Year was seen in (New Year's Eve is my elder sister Heather's birthday so New Year was seen in every year with a party) and finally Saturday January 3rd 1976 arrived and the Leeds United game. Notts had increased the admission prices for children from 30 pence to £1 and the school was closed for the holiday so no free tickets. Surely I wouldn't be stopped going again? Happily not and having parked the car Len, Mark and I joined the ever increasing queue on Meadow Lane, me with a £1 note firmly in my hand waiting for the turnstiles to open and as they did, I dropped my money. Panic set in as the queue started moving forwards and I scrambled around amongst the feet looking for the precious money. Thankfully I found it and was soon taking my place behind the dug outs as usual. The main thing I remember was the noise it was louder than I had ever heard anywhere and was both scary and fascinating in equal measure and when Leeds scored courtesy of Allan Clarke it got even louder. From what I remember it was a fabulous game and Notts were not disgraced but Leeds got a modicum of revenge for their League Cup defeat by winning 1:0 in front of 31192, the biggest crowd I had ever been in, and the bad news did not in any way stop there. When I got home I was told we were moving house again, as soon as we could sell going back to Worcester, 84 miles from Meadow Lane. I couldn't believe it I was absolutely distraught, my "love affair" over before it had begun but at least I was in Nottingham until we sold the house and that could take months. It didn't, the board was put up outside the front of the house on Monday 12th January1976 as I was leaving for school and as I got home later that afternoon I was told it was "Sold Subject to Contract" a couple from Sheffield had been driving down Brooklands Drive seen our house For Sale and wanted it and we were not exactly on a main road that's your luck. We were due to move back to Worcester on Monday 23rd February1976 I honestly don't think I have ever felt lower in my life, I still went to the few remaining home games including the friendly against Sheffield United and their manager was Jimmy Sirrel on FA Cup 4th Round day the 28th of January 1976. It resulted in a 3:0 win for Notts with goals from Les Bradd, Mick Vinter and an own goal from Paul Garner in front of 5545 supporters. The Notts fans gave a great reception both before and after the game to Jimmy. The days and weeks flew by and my last game finally arrived, Chelsea at home on Saturday February 21st 1976 with all their stars not a bad last game I guess and it certainly lived up to the billing Notts running out 3:2 winners with goals from Ian Scanlon, John Sims and Les Bradd having been behind twice. There was a leaving party at East Bridgford after the game (my Grandparents had moved there from Epperstone) and I am not ashamed to say I cried my eyes out and vowed there and then that one day I would be back in Nottingham again but until then I would maintain my support from afar.

We moved to Worcester and I was enrolled at Pitmaston Primary School and was just in time to take the 11 plus which they had stopped taking in Nottingham and amazingly I passed! So in September 1976 I started life at Worcester Royal Grammar School, a boy's only school, with about 800 pupils consisting mainly of day pupils but also some boarders from around the world such as Imran Khan the Pakistan cricketer turned politician. Having settled in I was happy and proud to tell anybody and everybody who asked that I was a Notts County supporter. Being so close to Birmingham the school was full of Aston Villa, West Brom, Wolves and Birmingham City supporters although there was a Luton Town fan, who like me came in for a lot of ribbing but, like me, was resolute in support of his team. My English teacher, Mr Goldfinch was a Charlton Athletic supporter and during my school years Notts and Charlton played each other regularly and we always had a 50 pence bet on the result. In the six years I was at school I paid out once and that was the very first year when Charlton won 1.0 at Meadow Lane in the last game of the season on May 14th 1977. He paid me back the following season when on Saturday 22nd October 1977 goals by Steve Carter and Mick Vinter secured a 2:0 win at Meadow Lane. The other eight meetings were all draws until Charlton got relegated at the end of the 1979/80 season but I won 50 pence in the FA Cup in the 1977/78 season when Mick Vinter scored twice in a 2 0 win at the Valley on Saturday 7th January 1978 (funnily enough by a quirk of fate I have never yet been to the Valley). I got into a routine at weekends going to watch Worcester City play every home game at St Georges Lane (St George's Lane is now a housing estate and Worcester City have no home ground of their own) just to get my "fix" of live football and I always hoped they would play Notts County in a cup match or a friendly or anything, I am still hoping to this day. I had a transistor radio glued to my ear listening to Radio 2 and every other week listened to the radio whilst watching Grandstand. Sunday was always Star Soccer with Hugh Johns. Then at the end of the 1975/76 season Hereford United were promoted to the old Division 2 so they would be playing Notts County and Edgar Street was only about 25 miles from where we lived surely I could go? You have guessed it............ predictable really, no I couldn't there was no one to take me on Saturday 23rd October 1976 and typically Notts won 4:1 with two goals from John Sims, one from Dave Needham and the other from Martyn Busby. Sadly four weeks later Saturday November 20th 1976, I was offered the chance to go to Edgar Street to watch Hereford play Oldham in a thrilling 0:0 draw. The outstanding memory being that the half time entertainment was the gentleman on the microphone encouraging the crowd to join in the singing of football songs such as "when the saints go marching in" and "blue is the colour" it was one of the longest half times I ever suffered. Even sadder though they played Forest as well on Wednesday March 2nd 1977 at Edgar Street and as it was a midweek game yes you have guessed it Dad took me and my sister Claire to the game in the Hereford end I am pleased to say sadly Forest won 1:0.

Regularly during the school holidays I spent some time in East Bridgford at my Grand Parents travelling up on the 144 bus from Worcester to Birmingham bus station, changing buses to the X99 from Birmingham to Nottingham Victoria bus station then the Skills bus to East Bridgford. So it was that I found myself there during the Easter Holidays in April 1979, when on the Wednesday (11th) there was a knock at the door. It was their next door neighbour Don (a Forest supporter) asking if I would like to go to the City Ground that evening to watch the European Cup Semi Final

First Leg against Cologne? He knew I was a Notts County fan. My initial reaction was "No Way" why watch them? But then I thought a European Cup Semi Final, when if ever would I get the chance again? Maybe it would be good to go? What to do? Don then said he had not got a ticket for me but was happy to take me if I wanted to go? If I did be ready for 5pm. What a dilemma! Could I? Should I? Not sure to this day if I am ashamed or not but at 5pm I was ready and waiting and on my way to the game. Having parked by 5:30pm Don and his friends went to the pub having arranged where to meet me after the game and I went in search of a ticket. Kick off was not until 7:30pm, that gave me two hours plenty of time surely? I went all the way round the ground and got the same answer "sorry sold out" "Sorry no tickets" and was just about to give up when a "ticket tout approached me with one ticket, great but how much? Amazingly he sold it to me for face value, "Adult" face value £6 and by 7:15pm I found myself inside the ground at the Bridgford Road end. It was packed I was 14 and not very tall, I am older now and not much taller, and I couldn't see a thing. Some kind person took sympathy on me and suggested he lift me up and sit me on the fence right next to the scoreboard. Suddenly I had the best view in the ground if a little precarious. When Cologne took the lead I did my best not to react but when they went 2 up I could not stop myself cheering, as you can imagine surrounded as I was, it did not go down well but there was no way I was going to support Forest. The game progressed and just past the hour Forest had turned it round completely and were now 3:2 up and I was getting a lot of ribbing although I must admit mostly friendly. There was one more sting in the tail though Cologne made a substitution bringing on a Japanese player called Yasuhiko Okudera and with less than ten minutes to go he equalised, I was delighted, as were the few Cologne fans there. Surely the second leg was a formality for the Germans? We all know the answer to that, sadly. A few days later heading home on the bus I was a jumble of mixed emotions, I felt guilty for "crossing the Trent" although I made it clear from the start I was a Notts fan. I felt pleased I had seen a great game of football and delighted Cologne had got a great result so back to the routine Worcester City one week Grandstand the next.

Worcester City at the time were quite a successful Non-League club having good FA Cup runs as well as successful league seasons and in the 1976/77 season they remained unbeaten until the last game of the season which was away at Barry Town losing 2:0 and in season 78/79 they all but got through to the 3rd round of the FA Cup beating Plymouth 2:0 at home in the 1st Round on Saturday 25th November. And drawing 0:0 away at Newport County (who had knocked out Hereford in the first round) in the 2nd Round on Saturday 16th December before drawing West Ham at home in the 3rd round. The draw was on the Saturday night in those days, if they won the replay. Going into injury time in the replay on the Monday evening December 18th Worcester were 1:0 up but Newport equalised and won in extra time and for good measure beat West Ham. It was exciting but not as good as watching Notts, but needs must.

On Saturday May 3rd 1980 aged 15, I finally got the opportunity to see Notts live again, getting permission to go with my best friend Paul to St Andrews Birmingham to see the last game of the season. It had been more than 1500 days since that Chelsea game at Meadow Lane and I was so excited in the days leading up to the game. We caught the train at Worcester Foregate Street to Birmingham New Street, then a bus to St Andrews (Paul knew Birmingham well so got us to the ground easily enough,) arriving there about 1pm. It was already very crowded. I had thought about wearing my black and white scarf but must admit I was glad I didn't. Birmingham really needed to win to guarantee promotion to Division 1 above Chelsea, Notts were in the bottom half of the table but safe from relegation. What a game it was in front of 33863 people and the television cameras as it was on Star Soccer on Sunday afternoon. Birmingham went 2:0 up Notts pulled it back to 2:2 with goals from Gordon Mair and Trevor Christie. Birmingham went in front again before Notts equalised again through Brian Kilcline and the game finished a draw 3:3. Chelsea did all they could beating Oldham 3:0 but once the season had finished Birmingham got promoted on goal difference from Chelsea with a difference of 6 goals.

The following season even from afar was a brilliant one culminating in promotion to Division one but also with Notts getting to the final of the Anglo Scottish Cup, although sadly not beating Chesterfield over two legs, losing the first leg at Saltergate 1:0 on Tuesday March 24th 1981 before conceding a 120th minute equaliser (after extra time) at home to draw on the night 1:1, Don Masson having squared the final and lose 2:1 on aggregate the following Tuesday March 31st 1981 in front of 12951. Finding information about the 2 matches as I still lived in Worcester was not exactly easy, Radio 2 hardly even mentioned it and there was very little in the Daily newspapers the next day. Notts visited Stamford Bridge on Saturday May 2nd 1981 and clinched promotion to the top flight of English Football for the first time in more than 56 years in front of 13324 supporters. Needless to say at 16, I had no way of going to the game so listened to my trusty radio and watched Grandstand to get the score. Notts won 2:0 with goals by Trevor Christie and Rachid Harkouk but as usual it was not as straight forward as that. The Chelsea fans invaded the pitch on several occasions and police horses came on the pitch at one stage to clear them it looked like the match would be abandoned but thankfully it wasn't and Notts were finally up with the big boys, I was delighted and gutted at the same time to have missed yet another big game. My time would come. On the Tuesday May 5th 1981 Notts played their final league game of the season at home to Cambridge United in front of a crowd of 12489 and won 2:0 with goals from Trevor Christie and Iain McCulloch but sadly I was not there again. The goals were shown on Midlands Today on the Wednesday evening, something I did not expect in Worcester.

More so than ever I was determined to see more games now we were playing the top sides in the country and it was not long before I got another chance. Aston Villa had won the league the season before and when the fixtures for 1981/82 season were announced in June their first league game of the season was at home to Notts County on Saturday August 29th, brilliant. I had been to St Andrews 18 months earlier, surely I could go to Villa Park? Have a guess! We were away on holiday only on the Gower Coast in Wales but it may as well have been Timbuktu as I had no chance of getting anywhere near Birmingham. I was really fed up even more so after the result Notts won 1:0 with a first half goal from Iain McCulloch. The fates had conspired against me again but school was fun the next term.

The year rolled by and in 1982 eventually I was leaving school with 7 O levels so surely heading back to live in Nottingham? Heading back yes, not to live at that time but to watch a match as now having passed my driving test in July 1982 I drove to watch the first game of the season on August 28th 1982 against John Toshack's Swansea City. The man had nothing nice to say about Notts County saying he "would not open his lounge curtains to watch them", it finished 0:0 but it was my first game at Meadow Lane in over 2370 days I was finally home and it was still as magical as ever, even though things had changed. The Meadow Lane End had been demolished in 1978 and replaced by a building which housed new dressing rooms and a social club but meant wooden planking to stand or sit on to watch the match.

Less than a month later I joined the Royal Navy on my 18th birthday September 19th 1982 starting basic training at HMS Raleigh having started to do A levels in History, Ancient History and Geography, if you please. But I got fed up with them so found myself even further away being based in Plymouth during basic training and moving to Portsmouth when I had qualified in the Electronic Warfare Branch but Notts County were still my life. I felt great sitting in the communal television room at HMS Raleigh in Plymouth on Saturday December 4th 1982 watching Match of the Day seeing Notts beat Forest 3:2 with goals from Iain McCulloch Paul Hooks and Trevor Christie and an awful miss from Willie Young thanks Willie Young. Having completed basic training I had the festive period back home in Worcester before joining HMS Dryad in January 1983 for specialist training finally flying to Gibraltar from Luton airport to join my first ship HMS Newcastle on Wednesday 18th May 1983 on the same flight as the Irish singers the Bachelors. I finally boarded the ship mid-afternoon and as my duties had not yet been allocated I was invited "ashore" for a few drinks by my new colleagues that evening and was more than happy to join them. After drinks in a few pubs we found ourselves at a pub known by all sailors (all experienced sailors anyway not new recruits like me) in Gibraltar called the Hole in T' Wall and it was run by a gentleman called Charles Trico, who was gay and extremely camp. That Wednesday night having been plied with drinks my ship mates "sold" me to Charles something that happened regularly to young sailors over the years it transpired later. I hadn't got a clue what was happening just went along with it at first! When I finally did understand what was happening I ran from the pub as fast as I could with laughter ringing in my ears and tried to find my way back to the ship with no clue where I was going. Good job Gibraltar is a small place. The Hole in t' Wall served its last drinks around about Wednesday 27th January 2016 more than forty years after Charles Trico had opened it and he now enjoys his retirement still in Gibraltar. Saturday21st May 1983 was FA Cup final day Brighton V Manchester United the pubs were open from 10am which was 9am English time and as I wasn't on duty it gave me another chance to get to know my new colleagues and to see Charles again. He thought it was hilarious but apologised and bought me a drink. So by the time of the final a good few drinks had been enjoyed and when it went into extra time there were even more drinks enjoyed. The pub I was in was divided equally by the ship's crew between Southerners supporting Brighton and Northerns cheering for United being a Midlander I admit I sided with the Northerners as well as one or two actual supporters of the clubs and a great afternoon was had by all. At the end of the game (it finished 2:2 after extra time Brighton taking the lead early in the first half to lead 1:0 at half time and equalising late on in the second half to force extra time) somebody found out I still have no idea how that Hull City (there were no Hull City supporters onboard) were on an end of season tour and were playing Gibraltar at the Victoria Stadium so off we all went the mile or so across the town drinks, in hand to watch Hull win 3:1 with goals from Brian Marwood, Billy Whitehurst and Billy Askew in front of a crowd of 5000. About 50 from the ship and a dozen actual Hull City fans were there and not all of us were arrested but one or three were. At half time the Hull players stayed on the pitch as it was so warm so we offered them some of our beer. Amazingly most, if not all, of them took a drink and why not. The ship sailed back to England on the Sunday morning and luckily the few miscreants from the football match had been released before the ship sailed. If we had missed the ship we would have had to pay our own way home. HMS Newcastle then stayed berthed in Portsmouth until June 1983 when we sailed for a 6 month Tour of Duty in the Falklands so I visited Nottingham a few days before we sailed, purchased my first replica shirt from Redmayne and Todd and proudly wore it whenever and wherever I could in those 6 months. I still have it somewhere as far as I know although I very much doubt it would fit me these days. Everywhere from Gibraltar and Ascension Island on the one month trip down to the South Atlantic to Port Stanley and South Georgia when we were on patrol I wore it. Having visited explorer Ernest Shackleton's grave on South Georgia during shore leave I joined in as members of the ships company played the Kings Own Border Regiment at football (as bad as I am at football it was a great laugh) in the deep snow only to be told afterwards we had been playing in a mine field, charming. In Dakar in Senegal, which we visited on the long journey home, whenever I had chance for a trip ashore the locals were treated to me wearing my Notts shirt. I spent one day along with a few colleagues as a guest of the British Ambassador in Dakar and proudly wore my shirt then.

The 1983/84 season started well The World Service (which I had learnt to rely on for all sports reports over the years) providing all the results each week as well as a commentary match. Notts opened their season on Saturday August 27th with a 4:0 win at Filbert Street against Leicester City with a goal from Martin O Neill and a hat trick from Trevor Christie but as my tour of duty continued things started to go badly. We did not win a game from Tuesday August 30th. Then we beat Birmingham City 2:1 at home with two goals the equaliser, then the winner from Rachid Harkouk, to go joint top of the League along with West Ham United, Aston Villa and Arsenal, but top on goals scored having scored one more goal than West Ham and both having a plus five goal difference, played two won two, until Saturday November 19th and a 2:0 win at Southampton with goals from Justin Fashanu and Trevor Christie a total of eleven matches which produced two draws at home to Stoke on October 22nd, when Brian Kilcline scored to give Notts the lead the other at home to Norwich on November 12th when Justin Fashanu scored to give Notts the lead. so just two points. By the time I got home on December 19th we were 18th in the league having just lost to Liverpool at Anfield 5:0.

Six months is a long time to be away from home and many things had changed by the time I got home again but the one that stood out the most was that car registrations had changed from three letters, three numbers and a letter (VNP700G) to a letter three numbers three letters (A476RDS) Sad I know. On Boxing Day Notts were at home to Luton Town with an 11:30am kick off and with a match at Old Trafford the next day. You couldn't see today's overhyped over paid Premiership players doing that this was only just over 34 years ago, how times change. So I drove up with my friend Adrian the Luton Town supporter from school. We parked outside the Trent Navigation and went in for a drink before the game. There I met a lady called Loraine, who was in time going to be my wife and mother of my children. That was the only good thing about that particular day as Luton ran out easy 3:0 winners. Amazingly the next day Notts got a very creditable 3:3 draw at Old Trafford having been 2:0 and 3:1 down with a penalty from Trevor Christie and two goals in the last 10 minutes from Justin Fashanu. I headed back down to Portsmouth at the end of the Christmas holidays but from then on all my leave periods and weekends off were spent either driving up to Nottingham or catching the train to be in Sherwood with Loraine and of course at Meadow Lane.

The FA Cup Quarter Final at home to Everton on Saturday 10th March 1984 stands out, Notts fans were moved out of the County Road Stand and put in the Kop. It poured with rain all day so the Notts fans got soaked and Everton won 2:1, John Chiedozie getting an early equaliser after Kevin Richardson had put Everton ahead before Andy Gray scored the winner just after half time with a header about a foot off the ground. After many years of frustration I was finally able to watch Notts fairly regularly just as they started falling down the leagues. Mine and Loraine's first away game together was at Kenilworth Road Luton on April 21st 1984 (my Mums 42nd birthday) and what an eventful day it was. I drove and we parked on Kenilworth Road itself, getting a parking ticket for our troubles. We left after John Chiedozie had made the game 2:2 late in the game Trevor Christie earlier equalising for the first time and missed the winning goal that Luton scored in injury time. We never left a game early after that.

We got engaged on 2nd June 1984 on my younger older sister Claire's wedding day. I had been a naughty boy on board HMS Newcastle and had been punished by 14 days stoppage of leave and having already missed my oldest sister Heather's wedding, as I was on my way to the Falklands in 1983 when she got married on August 29th, although I did send a "Good Wishes" cassette recorded in Gibraltar, it appeared I would miss this one too. I appealed to the Captain and was granted leave from 4am on Saturday morning 2nd June to 4pm Sunday afternoon 3rd June 1984 so duly drove home from Portsmouth to Worcester after finishing my shift on the "middle" watch midnight to 4am without any sleep. I flagged a milk float down on

Birdlip Hill in Gloucestershire for a pint of milk to keep me going on the way. The poor bloke had no idea what was happening but happily sold me a pint when I explained. By the time I got to the ceremony I was more than tired having been awake since 7am on the Friday morning and in a "moment of madness" proposed to Loraine Tto which she saidyes. While we were in the car. She had travelled down to Worcester from Nottingham and we were married at St Paul's church in Daybrook on Saturday August 3rd 1985, NOT in the football season but Notts were playing a home friendly against Ipswich which they drew 1:1. Ian McParland equalising in the 33rd minute a goal in the 28th minute by Kevin Wilson. I left HMS Newcastle in May 1985 joining HMS Nelson after eight weeks of leave in Nottingham Of course this was all in the close season. While at HMS Nelson, I had the luck to meet Bobby Stokes the ex Southampton footballer who scored the winning goal in the 1976 FA Cup Final against Manchester United and what a gentleman he was. He was more than happy to chat about his footballing career and that goal. Sadly he is no longer with us passing away in May 1995 at the age of just 44.

We were at Meadow Lane on Easter Monday 6th May 1985 when Manchester City came to town. Notts needed to win to stand any chance of staying up and City needed to win in their promotion battle. Notts were 3 up by half time with goals by Justin Fashanu, Rachid Harkouk and Alan Young. The City fans upset by the score tried to wreck the ground and get the game abandoned some even managing to get down the tunnel and into the City dressing room. Both Billy McNeill and Jimmy Sirrell the respective managers came on the pitch at half time appealing for calm and telling the Manchester City fans if the problems continued the game would be abandoned and Notts would be awarded the result 3:0! After half an hour the second half was able to commence. Needless to say this affected the Notts players and City pulled 2 goals back in the second half. Thankfully only the two but at the end of the season a week later they were still promoted and Notts were still relegated losing 1:0 at Craven Cottage but all that paled into insignificance with the disaster that unfolded at Valley Parade Bradford that weekend of 11th May 1985. On what was supposed to be a day of celebration as Bradford were awarded the Third Division Trophy in their last home game of the season against Lincoln City the main stand caught fire and with it being wooden and there being years' worth of litter underneath it within minutes the whole stand was engulfed in flames killing 56 and seriously injuring 265 people who had just gone to watch a football match. Men women and children all perished. On Tuesday 3rd September 1985 Loraine and I drove to Belle Vue Doncaster for the Milk Cup first round second leg match. Notts held a 1:0 lead from the first leg with a goal from David Clarke and as we left Nottingham it was a lovely sunny evening but by the time we parked at Doncaster it was raining we had no coats in the car so Loraine grabbed a Gents black steel tipped umbrella I grabbed a Notts County flag and we headed to the turnstiles. I was told to put the flag back in the car or have it taken off me as an "offensive weapon" Loraine just walked in with the umbrella very strange Notts lost the game 2:1 having taken the lead through Mark Goodwin but went through on away goals after extra time.

In November 1985 I joined HMS Avenger based in Plymouth and in February 1986, I sailed for a six month tour of duty in the Caribbean as West Indies guard ship again relying on The World Service again for all sports news and results, visiting Belize, The Turks and Caicos Islands the most fabulous Islands I had or have ever been to, completely unspoilt by man and with very few inhabitants and beautiful sandy beaches, a real paradise. Nassau in The Bahamas as well as Corpus Christi in Texas where I learnt to my amazement that the legal age for marriage with parental consent was 14 as a lady I was chatting to told me her 14 year old daughter was getting married that weekend and she was delighted and asked if I would like to attend. I declined. Is it still the same? No thankfully it is now 16 (I am led to believe) with parental consent which makes all the difference in the world but how sad. I then visited Norfolk in Virginia where I made the biggest mistake of my whole naval career, or one of them. I was on watch from 4am to 8am, the morning watch. We were anchored off Norfolk waiting to sail into port and like everybody else I was looking forward to some "shore time" having been at sea for a few weeks, when the Officer of the Watch radioed to me and asked me to identify a certain vessel on a certain bearing (well it was my job) I took a quick look and replied a fishing vessel Sir nothing to worry about. As dawn broke the Officer of the Watch called me onto the bridge and showed me my "fishing vessel". It was the USS NIMITZ at the time one of the biggest aircraft carriers in the world. Luckily the Officer of the Watch had a sense of humour and no real harm was done but I was ribbed about it for the rest of the tour. Norfolk in Virginia boasts a much larger Naval Base, in area, larger than the county of Nottinghamshire, being the largest Naval base in the world and covering approximately 3400 acres or 248.6 square miles. It was also while in Norfolk I discovered why American military personnel have so many medals on their chests, In any film you see. They give their ships medals the same ones they award to the crew painting them on the funnel and the crew get a medal for crossing the Atlantic and another for serving a year onboard ship they are two medals I never received. We also spent a few days alongside in West Palm Beach in Florida. I went to the beach with a couple of mates and we were throwing a rugby ball around. The sea appeared to be full of "inflatable condoms" but no people and not knowing what they were we took the ball in with us and larked around. Someone threw the ball close to me I dived to catch it and felt the most amazing pain I have ever felt in my thigh and leg. I had no idea what it was but ran out of the sea screaming in pain and with "tentacles attached to my shorts and legs. The "inflatable condoms" were Portuguese Men of War jellyfishes whose sting can be deadly. I was all for dropping my shorts but a local asked my mates if either of them wanted a wee, as the urine neutralises the sting I am not sure if it was a good or bad thing but they did not (I have been told many years later that urine does not work anyway) so I had to limp back to the ship about a mile away and by the time I got back my thigh and leg had swollen up to twice its normal size. Luckily the doctor was onboard and he gave me some cream and tablets that took the pain away and by the morning the swelling had gone down a lot as well. In West Palm Beach and in every other port I proudly wore my shirt although when I mentioned Nottingham the only things people knew about or had heard of about Nottingham were Robin Hood and Brian Clough, oh well I tried. Before I had sailed we signed for a house in Daybrook and Loraine moved in while I was away, spending six months on her own but with family fairly close by if she needed anything. I think she did a fabulous job and it was very strange when I got home going into a new house, but I soon got used to it.

I left HMS Avenger on September 22nd and after a short period of leave In October 1986 I was posted to HMS Heron in Yeovil (RNAS Yeovilton) travelling down by car on Tuesday 14th. I arrived early afternoon to be told I was going to be doing main gate security but was not rostered on until Wednesday 15th in the afternoon. Having unpacked and found my bed in a six bed mess deck on the edge of the runway used by those on main gate security it was great after a night shift trying to sleep with Harrier jump jets taking off and landing all day as well as all sorts of other aircraft and helicopters. I turned the car round and drove back to Nottingham for the Benefit Match against Forest. Sadly I had missed the meeting at the Astoria on the 15th September to which 1500 people attended, with many more locked outside, because Notts County had debts of £2 million and the directors were thinking of putting the club into liquidation. At the meeting players directors and supporters pledged to carry on with the financial support and Lifeline was established. It is still going strong. I joined Lifeline and I am still a member. Mr Clough had suggested before the game the crowd could be as high as 15000+ but Notts County secretary Neil Hook was more conservative hoping the crowd would be around 10000. Sadly on a damp but mild night only 3299 people turned up at Meadow Lane about half of them from across the Trent. A very disappointing attendance after the turn out at the Astoria a month earlier. Forest ran out 5:2 winners with Garry Birtles scoring 4 and Gary Mills the other for Forest with David Clarke and Richard Young replying for Notts. Although the result was not the important factor that night the money raised which I believe was about £14,000, was the most important thing. The following evening there was a Save our Soccer Cabaret at the Meadow Club with Jimmy Sirrel Neal Hooks and the players in attendance along with the Lord Mayor and Lady Mayoress. The club was full of supporters and the aim was to raise another £2000+. It featured 5 bands and was headlined by local band Paper Lace but sadly I missed that to as I was back at Yeovilton. (I have tried all I can to find out who the other 4 bands were even putting an appeal out on Paul Robey's show on BBC Radio Nottingham but sadly nobody seems to know).

While I was based at Yeovilton on main gate security I had a "run in" with Prince Andrew and not in a pleasant way. He tried to get me into trouble for doing my job properly, but it has to be said I came out of it far better than he did. New Year's Eve 1986 at midnight found me stood at the Main Gate at HMS Heron and to say it was quiet would be an understatement,

I saw absolutely nobody and no vehicles for an hour either side of midnight but it did mean that at 1am I was allowed to go home on leave and was tucked up in bed in Nottingham by dawn. A great way to start the year and a Mickey Waitt hat trick at home to Gillingham in a 3:1 win on Saturday 3rd January 1987 made things even better. It got better nine months later as our son Daniel was born on Thursday 10th September 1987 at the City Hospital. Loraine was in hospital in labour as England were playing West Germany on the Wednesday evening and the television room was next door to her room so it was "you alright?" then back to the television to watch all the way through the game. England lost 3:1 with Gary Lineker scoring just before half time but by then England were already two goals behind so no surprise there. As there was still no sign of our son once the England game had finished I went home to wash and change and popped in my local club on the way to tell everybody how things were going and of course for a pint maybe more. Back to hospital after closing time still no progress it was gone midnight now but nothing. Finally the staff decided Loraine would have to have a Caesarean Section so took her off to theatre, amazingly I was allowed to be there and watched as they cut her open pulled Daniel out and passed him to me. I must admit the first thing I did was to check he had five fingers on each hand and five toes on each foot but I forgot to look for the three sixes. It was just gone 5am by now and like Loraine or maybe not quite as bad I was shattered, but at 9am I was at Notts County enrolling him in the Junior Magpies. The club were kind enough to send Ian McParland and Dave Thompson to the hospital to have photographs taken. The hospital were delighted with this because at the same time a 55 year old woman with her 65 year old husband had given birth to a baby making her the oldest woman to have a baby in Britain at that time and they were looking for a reason to take the spotlight off her.

On Saturday 12 September 1987 Notts played away at Northampton Town winning 1:0 with Gary Lund scoring. On Saturday December 5th 1987 Notts faced Port Vale at Vale Park in the second round of the FA Cup, the route wasn't as easy as it is now and we got lost on the way before spotting some other Notts supporters in a car and attempting to follow them. I think it must have been Nigel Mansell, who was driving the speed they were going at but somehow we kept them in sight long enough to get back to civilisation. We then found our own way to the ground only to suffer a 2:0 defeat. The following Saturday, December 12th, I was home again and Notts were away at Port Vale in the league this time so feeling more confident that we knew the way we went again this time taking Mik with us. On the way I had problems with the car and somehow ran out of water in the radiator Mik and I saw a farm in the distance and with plastic bottles in hand set off across the fields to ask for some water. On the way across the fields we had to go under an electric fence used to keep the livestock in place, I did not duck low enough and my backside touched the fence giving me a shock. Very painful but I think as a farmer's son maybe my pride hurt more than my backside Mik thought it was hilarious as did Loraine when I got back to the car. Mobile again we got to Vale Park and this time won 3:1 with two goals from Ian McParland and one from Geoff Pike. Amazing what a difference a week makes.

On Saturday September 10th 1988, on Daniel's first birthday, Notts played Northampton again this time at home so having left the Royal Navy, Loraine and I took him to his first match at Meadow Lane in the County Road Stand Z Block and you have guessed it this time Northampton won 1:0. On Saturday March 19th 1988 Loraine and I drove up to Roker Park for a top of the table clash with Sunderland. We parked in the huge car park to the side of the ground and went for a drink in the Social Club nearby. It was very friendly but as we were wearing colours there was plenty of banter but no hint of trouble. By the end of the match things had changed a bit Notts had got a very dubious equalizer courtesy of Paul Barnes to make it 1:1 and the natives were getting restless. At the final whistle the Notts fans were kept behind for a good half an hour then were given a police escort towards the sea front where the coaches were parked. I told a policemen we were parked in the car park pointing at our car and his reply was "get as close to your car as you can and run like f@@k", charming. In 2016 Angie, my second wife and I went to stay at her cousins apartment in Roker overlooking the North Sea, Roker Park is now a housing estate. How times change.

On Tuesday April 19th 1988 Loraine and I went to Molineux for the Associate Members Cup Semi Final South 2nd Leg having drawn 1:1 at home with a goal from Ian McParland and with a chance of Wembley for the winners Wolves were a division below us but had a player called Steve Bull. For the one and only time we went by train on a "football special" and I have to say that Wolverhampton station is one of the most intimidating places I have ever been in my life and with a distinct lack of police it felt even less safe. Wolves won easily 3:0 I would hate to think what would have happened if they had lost.

Life moved on I settled into civilian life and having tried one or two jobs, I got a job as a bus driver for Nottingham City Transport, shift work but with the opportunity to take in more games at Meadow Lane and away from home. On Saturday August 19th 1989 I drove with Loraine to Brisbane Road for the first game of the season against Leyton Orient. As usual we arrived with plenty of time parked up and found a pub full of Notts fans and had a coke or two and enjoyed the banter. It was a beautiful sunny day and they were serving alcohol inside the ground which you could sit and drink on the terraces. Notts ran out 1:0 winners courtesy of a first half goal from Phil Stant and so to the journey home. We were going to head for the North Circular then round to the M1 but were not exactly sure of the way. Another Notts fan in a car suggested we follow him, which we duly did, and as we turned up a street with windows open as it was so warm we heard someone shout "this is a one way street and you going the wrong way". Great but we were committed now so on we went and up another street you have guessed it another one way street the wrong way and at the top of this street there was a police car. They stopped us needless to say but where the others had gone I had no idea. I explained we were lost and trying to reach the North Circular hoping for the best, but fearing the worst, but amazingly the policeman having explained what we were doing wrong gave us directions and sent us on our way. I can only assume our accent not being local worked in our favour. Whatever it was I did not need telling twice. I thanked him and we left with a note to myself never to accept help or directions from Notts fans again, if the two incidents today and at Port Vale were anything to go by.

On Wednesday 28th March 1990 Loraine (6 months pregnant) and I travelled to Twerton Park Bath to watch Notts play Bristol Rovers in The Associates Members Cup Southern Area Final 1st Leg again, with a first ever visit to Wembley again the elusive prize. At the time Bristol Rovers were third in the league and Notts fourth six points below them. It was a good game considering what was at stake Rovers edging it 1:0 with a 78th minute goal from David Mehew. All to play for in the second leg at Meadow Lane on Monday 2nd April or so we thought. Step forward referee Mr Brian Hill. Need I say more! Yet again robbed of a first ever trip to Wembley, but we did not have to wait much longer. On Sunday May 27th 1990 Notts County got to Wembley for the first time in their history, against Tranmere in the Division Three Play Off Final having had a fabulous season and finishing third in the league behind a pair of Bristols. The Play Off Semi Final first leg was at Burnden Park Bolton on Sunday 13th May and I took family and friends up in a mini bus. Notts got a 1:1 draw, Gary Lund equalising before half time so we drove away from the ground in high spirits only for the mini bus to be "bricked" as we drove under a foot bridge. Luckily nobody was hurt but we were all badly shaken. So to the Second Leg at Meadow Lane on Wednesday 16th May 1990 with Notts running out 2:0 winners with goals from Tommy Johnson and Kevin Bartlett and finally we had booked our first ever trip to Wembley. I queued overnight outside Meadow Lane on Friday 18th May to get tickets not because we would sell out but because it felt the right thing to do. There were probably a couple of dozen of us spent the night there talking laughing and joking none of us really knowing why we were doing it but all of us wanting to and by the time the ticket office opened there were hundreds more people in the queue. Loraine was 8 months pregnant at the time of the final and we agreed if it was another boy we would name him after the Notts goalscorer/s in the final. I ran a 15 seater mini bus for family and friends even taking a Forest supporter Gerald Goodale (to show us the way lol) why not. The M1 was a plethora of Notts and Tranmere fans black and white and blue and white everywhere and all was going well until just past Northampton whilst in the fast lane I heard a bang. The back wheels were a twin axle and the inside of the two tyres on the nearside had a blow out. This was below the seat Loraine was sitting on. We made it over to the hard shoulder and I sent Loraine to find an emergency telephone, they are no more than a mile apart on any motorway, as I looked for the spare tyre which was on a rack underneath the bus but was rusted solid. Eventually I got it out got the damaged tyre off and put the new one on. Then in my frustration as time was passing I threw the punctured tyre down the embankment thought better of it and had to retrieve it. The whole time we were being hooted by other supporter of both clubs which made me even more annoyed. By now I was black and black but we were mobile again. Our initial plan had been to park in the car park of The Corner House pub in Edgeware less than a mile walk from Stanmore Tube Station and have a drink or two before making our way to the stadium, but as we were so late we parked at Stanmore just outside the tube station and caught the tube to Wembley. Even at my age (I was 25) the first view of the Twin Towers sent a tingle down my spine it was magical, a dump but magical. We walked up Wembley Way but sadly we didn't have much time to enjoy the atmosphere but went on to have a fabulous day as you all know winning 2:0 with goals from Tommy Johnson and Craig Short so if the new baby was a boy he was going to be called Tommy Craig. Kimberley was born 25 days later again at the City Hospital but far quicker. Loraine's water's broke in Wilkinson's in Sherwood at 9:30am on Thursday 21st of June 1990 and our daughter appeared via Emergency Forceps by 11am. A year later on Sunday June 2nd 1991 Notts were at Wembley again after another wonderful season this time finishing fourth in Division Two. The first leg of the Semi Final of the Play Offs was away at Ayresome Park Middlesbrough on Sunday May 19th 1991 and Notts got a 1:1 draw with Captain Phil Turner scoring first before a late equaliser. I had bet on Notts that day £20 on Turner to score first and Notts to win 2:1 it would have won me several hundred pounds and Notts had more than enough chances to win by that score. I was gutted and have never bet on Notts since. The second leg at Meadow Lane on Wednesday 22nd May 1991 was a very nervy affair, Notts eventually running out 1:0 winners with a late goal from Paul Harding so on Sunday June 2nd 1991 we were heading to Wembley again this time against Brighton in the Division Two Play Off Final with a place in the top division of English football the prize. Once again I ran a mini bus for family and friends although Dan and Kim again stayed at Loraine's parents and this time everything ran smoothly and we were parked in The Corner House car park by 11am enjoying the atmosphere of a very large pub full of football supporters before again catching the tube to Wembley the whole day went perfectly including the result Notts running out 3:1 winners with two goals from Tommy Johnson and another from Dave Regis giving us a three goal lead before Brighton got a late goal back and Notts were back in the top division for the first time in seven seasons. In researching this book I asked all my friends and fellow Notts fans if they could remember the name of the pub and got about twenty different answers so made the effort to drive to Edgeware to find out for myself and was shocked to find out the pub The Corner House is now a "drive through" Mcdonalds restaurant and the large car park is now a petrol station. Progress I guess?

In June 1991 the fixtures were published. Unlike our game against the League Champions on their own pitch when we were drawn away to Aston Villa in August 1991, as the first game in the top division, this time we did not get the Champions who were Arsenal but only Manchester United who had finished 6th in the league but had won the European Cup Winners Cup the previous May beating Barcelona 2:1 in Rotterdam at Old Trafford on Saturday August 17th. That would do I guess? I drove with Mik Wyer accompanying me and sadly Notts ran in to a player called Andrei Kanchelskis who had made his debut for Manchester United in the penultimate game of the previous season on May 11th 1991 at Selhurst Park against Crystal Palace. He was so fast nothing and nobody could stop him and Notts suffered as many more teams were going to this season eventually slipping to a 2:0 defeat with goals from Mark Hughes and Bryan Robson although with no bitterness at all maybe, just maybe the referee was the slightest bit biased. But on the other hand maybe it could and probably should have been much worse.

About 8am one Monday morning in March 1992 as Loraine was getting Daniel ready for school and trying to feed Kimberley the house phone rang. I answered it and the lady on the other end said "this is Central Television here a couple have pulled out of quiz show Bullseye as you are on the "local reserve" list would you like to take their place?" I had written to Central Television when Bullseye moved from Birmingham to Nottingham a couple of years earlier expressing a desire to appear on the show. Not having heard anything I had forgotten all about that letter until I received this phone call. Without asking Loraine I said "yes absolutely" to which the lady said "be at the Central Television studios for midday you can bring someone with you if you want? To sit in the audience" then as I put the phone down and told Loraine the panic set in. What to do with the children? Who to take with us? As usual her parents were fabulous. Her dad agreed to sit with the children and her mum came with us. Once parked at the studios, Loraine's mum came by bus later,. We were taken straight to the canteen for lunch with the other contestants. They filmed two shows a day for thirteen days and they also filmed a Christmas special so it was very intensive. Competing against us on the same show were a couple of lads from Mansfield and another couple. After lunch we were taken into the studios for a dress rehearsal and a "dummy run" so the dart players (Loraine) could get used to the board and the people answering the questions (me) could get used to where they were sitting, then it was time to change and go into make up if required and we were on. I wore a Notts tie and Jim Bowen being a Blackburn supporter gave me plenty of good natured ribbing about my choice of team. Loraine did really well with her darts I let her down with answers to questions, I didn't know who Nancy Astor was or why she was so significant, I do now and in the faces round none of us knew Norma Major, we eventually finished third (ok last) with a couple of hundred pounds. As the adverts approached we were given our bendy bullies, goblet tankard and darts. I still have my tankard and bully. Keith Deller was the dart player throwing for charity and he raised £330 doubled to £660 for the lads from Mansfield who won and they donated it to a local special care baby unit. They went on to win the Star Prize a holiday to Florida (I think) it was certainly a holiday. They had and took the option after the show of taking money to the price of the holiday. We were also given £150 each travelling expenses from Daybrook to Lenton Lane and were invited into the Green Room for as much food and drink as we wanted. There we met up again with the contestants from the other show and their dart player Cliff Lazarenko as well as Jim Bowen and Tony Green! What a gentleman Jim Bowen was. Loraine's mum was also there and she told us that between recordings the audience all moved seats just in case anybody watching at home recognised the same person in the same seat in two shows. A fabulous day was had by all and it has been repeated a few times on Challenge TV over the years but sadly we have not received any repeat fees. Can't grumble that much though I think we did very well financially out of the whole day.

After the last home game of the 1991/92 season on Saturday May 2nd a 2:1 home win over Luton Town in front of 11380 with Rob Matthews scoring twice after Luton had taken an early lead through Julian James and which ultimately ended with both clubs being relegated to the second tier the County Road and Spion Kop stands were demolished and rebuilt during the close season! Every week on a Friday the family went down to see how the building work was progressing and like everybody were amazed when the new stands were officially opened with the visit of Leicester City on Saturday August 22nd! A game that finished in a 1:1 draw a David Smith penalty equalising for Notts a goal by Phil Gee in front of 10502.

Life got better I managed to work my shifts so I was driving buses from Sunday to Friday and no late duties so got Saturday's off and Loraine and I watched Notts home and away initially leaving Daniel and Kimberley with Loraine's parents but it wasn't long before we were travelling as a family all over the country. On Sunday August 16th 1992 I took Daniel to his first away game at St Andrews Birmingham even though it was live on television, the first time Notts County had ever been involved in a live television match Birmingham won 1:0 with an early goal by Louie Donowa. On Tuesday 24th August 1993 we took both of them to Boothferry Park Hull, our first away trip as a family, for the Coca Cola League Cup 1st round 2nd leg against Hull City having won the 1st leg at Meadow Lane 2:0 with goals from Gary Lund and Paul Cox the week before. We drove there as usual and with a crowd of 2222 watched as Notts lost 3:1 a Mark Draper goal saving Notts after Hull had gone 3:0 up and putting Notts through on the away goal rule.

In November 1994 I fulfilled one of my life's ambitions, (sort of) I had and still have always wanted to visit all 92 Football League Clubs with Notts County but since 1987 a club has been relegated from the Football League and one promoted making the 92 clubs different each year this changed to two up two down in 2003 making it even more difficult so on Friday November 18th I set off with two colleagues from Nottingham City Transport, Stafford Watson and Terry Bostock (sadly no longer with us) and another Notts fan and good friend Mik Wyer (sadly no longer with us) to visit all 132 English Scottish and Welsh League Clubs in seven days raising money for BBC Children in Need. The plan was to start at the City Ground and finish at Meadow Lane a week later. The driving being shared between myself Terry and Stafford as Mik had no licence so was mainly navigator (no Sat Nav in those days). In the weeks and months beforehand as the journey was planned Stafford arranged the free hire of mini bus and we all got companies to sponsor us and put their logos on the side of the van Nottingham City Transport arranged for us to stop at bus depots throughout the country to refuel and Notts County were kind enough to donate some first team shirts for us to travel in numbered 2 3 4 and 5 and including Sir Charlie Palmer's famous shirt when he scored the winning goal at Meadow Lane against Forest in a 2:1 win on February 12th 1994, Gary McSwegan opening the scoring in front of 17911. Amazingly it was Charlie's first league goal since the opening day of the 1990/91 season on August 25th 1990 when he scored the opening goal at Hull City Gary Lund getting the winner in a 2:1 win and his first goal for the club since he opened the scoring in a 1:1 home draw against Barnsley in the Preliminary Round of the Anglo Italian Cup in a game that finished 1:1 on Tuesday 15th September 1992. Charlie is still a legend and always will be and February 12th is affectionately known as Sir Charlie Palmer Day to ALL Notts County fans. The AA had given us a route from club to club starting at Forest and going South but we were going North so by reading it backwards it helped a bit (NOT) Even "Captain Cash" from the News of the World sponsored us and we appeared on his page in the paper on Sunday 20th. The big drawback to this was that for the picture that appeared in the paper we had to wear Forest scarves and Bobble Hats at the City Ground but luckily the picture was in Black and White and it was for charity. Larry Lloyd was there to see us off from the City Ground just after 9am on Friday 18th and I drove out the car park heading for Field Mill Mansfield then Sincil Bank Lincoln and Saltergate Chesterfield and on up the Eastern side of the country. Whenever we arrived at a ground in the daylight or the dark, and with it being November there was a lot of dark, a picture was taken off the ground with the club name showing and one of us asked directions to the next planned club. We had planned the route and where to stop each night but maybe because it was new and different and maybe because we had no idea what the next few days would bring we drove further than planned that first day, eventually parking up in the early hours of the Saturday morning outside Ayresome Park Middlesbrough. We slept as best as we could in the van but we soon realised this was not going to be either easy or comfortable. When we woke a few hours later we realised that Stadium Security had been watching us all night and as we were waking they bought us all a cup of coffee. Very kind of them even more so when they let us into the ground to use the facilities for a wash and to brush our teeth. Off we went finishing the North East and by 2:15ish we were pulling in to Shielfield Park the home of Berwick Rangers. I t was match day and they were at home to Clyde. We were greeted by the Berwick Commercial Manager Ian Davison who offered us tickets for the game which we sadly declined because of our tight schedule but we did promise we would return at a later date with our families. Berwick won the game that day 2:1. Consequently on March 30th 1996 we returned to Shielfield Park as Guests of Honour to watch them play Clyde again. Charlie Nicholas was playing for Clyde by now and on the journey to Berwick we visited the Hillsborough memorial at Anfield laying flowers and scarves. It was an excellent game with Clyde running out 3:2 winners. Mr Davison still gave us a tour of the ground before we left, including the dressing rooms and the boardroom fabulous hospitality. On we drove across the border through Edinburgh and further North and at about 7:30pm we found ourselves in the small village of St Michaels which lies next door to the more well known St Andrews very appropriate we thought with one of our party called Mik. As it was the first ever National Lottery draw in the next half hour we decided to stop for a comfort break and watch the draw. Amazingly none of us won the jackpot, in fact nobody did that night, so back to the van. We pressed on Northwards to Dundee and the closest two grounds in Britain approximately 200 yards apart although I paced it at 179 paces which makes their nearest point just a bit closer. On we went into the Highlands finally parking about 2am. This time at Dingwall outside Ross County's ground and again we slept as well as we could, needless to say little better than the previous night. Sunday morning dawned we took our pictures and as we found nowhere to wash we decided to head South again before we finally came across a Little Chef so we stopped for breakfast and to recharge Mik's video camera as discreetly as possible and for a wash before heading on into Fife. We stopped at Firs Park, the home of East Stirlingshire in a street of terraced houses as we stopped one of the doors opened and a man came running out with a copy of the News of the World and asked us all to sign it for him. Fame at last. On we went later in the day parking up at Cliftonhill the home of Albion Rovers. We parked next to a grassy mound and standing on it we could see the whole ground. It is a tiny ground with a small main stand and a small wall no higher than four feet running round the rest of the ground. As we took our pictures we watched as half a dozen youngsters threw their ball over the wall and climbed over after it to play on the pitch. You could see that happening at Old Trafford NOT but more interestingly for me why did anybody pay to watch the match when you could stand where we were and watch the whole game free. There was nobody around to ask so when I got home curiosity got the better of me and I rang up to enquire. Their answer was that they employed security guards to move on anybody who was standing outside watching. Glasgow and Celtic Park the home of Celtic is a very impressive stadium. We were even allowed to have our pictures taken with a replica of the European Cup, which they won in Lisbon in 1967 then came Ibrox the home of Rangers in its way as impressive a stadium as Celtic Park but very different in design. We parked in the car park at one end and as I had already noticed the 5 a side pitches across the road from the stadium were in use and there were a few people watching, I went to ask directions to Kilbowie Park Clydebank our next ground. As the other three took pictures. I asked a very nice gentleman who smiled at me and said his name was John Steadman and he was the Clydebank Chairman. Amazing he then suggested when we got there to go in the Social Club and tell the staff he had sent us. As I was thanking him I heard a commotion across the street in the car park and as I ran off to see what was happening I saw the other three racing across the car park to the wall at the edge of the car park after two young lads. The charmless pair had broken into the mini bus and gone through our possessions. Mik was all but up with them when without hesitating they jumped the wall. It was not very high no more than two feet this side but luckily Mik or the others did not follow, as there was at least a fifteen foot drop the other side. We regrouped at the bus. The side door window had been smashed but it appeared nothing had been taken. What a relief but we were all fuming, we were doing this for people like them. The police were called and were more than helpful although they told us there was little they could do they escorted us to a glaziers who very kindly repaired the window for free and shaken we drove to Clydebank. Inside the Social Club it was clear they had been expecting us they gave us a meal of burger and chips and a pint each, as well as giving us a Clydebank mug each and offering us the chance to stay the night. That seemed like a great idea but as we had already fallen behind schedule with our problems at Ibrox we declined and once we had finished our meals and drinks we set off again. Irony of ironies in September 2012 with my second wife Angie we were on a touring holiday of Scotland when our car broke down on the outskirts of Glasgow. We managed to limp to a garage to get the car repaired and the garage manager turned out to be John Steadman's son who sadly informed me his father had passed away and asked if I wouldn't mind paying for the meals and drinks we had had that night seventeen years ago. Luckily he was only joking but what a small world. We found ourselves in Greenock and as we approached Cappielow we passed a fish and chip shop called Zavaronis'. I was led to believe it was run by child star Lena Zavaroni's family Lena was born in 1973 in Greenock and won Television talent show Opportunity Knocks at 10 years of age having been told that in 1984, when I was in the Navy and in Faslane for a few days when we had had a night out in Greenock. So having taken pictures of the ground on the way back out of Greenock towards Ayr United we stopped and bought some Haggis as none of us had ever tried it before. On we went not getting as far as Ayr because we were just too exhausted and eventually parking as usual in the early hours at Rugby Park Kilmarnock. Monday morning whilst taking pictures I chatted to the groundsman and explained to him what we were doing and the connection between our two clubs the great Iain McCulloch who joined Notts from Kilmarnock in 1978 and he kindly offered us the use of the home dressing room to shower and clean up our first proper shower since Friday morning. They had got a 0:0 draw with Celtic on the Saturday and the dressing room was still very untidy including a couple of programmes which he kindly let us have and he also let us walk down the tunnel to the edge of the pitch. Sad but fun. Now feeling more refreshed than at any time since Friday morning on we went to Ayr then Stranraer and Queen of the South before heading towards England again through Gretna Green then heading for Carlisle. We were a bit behind schedule but when we got to Gretna Green we heard bagpipes as somebody was getting married so decided to stop and take a look round and catch time up later so we spent half an hour or so looking round and taking pictures before setting off finally back into England. We went down the West of England and made steady progress all day but still didn't arrive at Maine Road Manchester until about 9:30pm, we had learnt our lesson from Glasgow and I stayed in the van while the others quickly got out and took pictures Moss Side is no place for strangers at the best of time and certainly not after dark. We arrived at Goodison Park, Everton about midnight they had played Liverpool earlier in the evening winning 2:0 and all we could say was there was rubbish everywhere. On we drove finally arriving at the Racecourse Ground Wrexham and parking for the night tempers were fraying we were all exhausted and we were barely half way. Whose bloody idea was this! Tuesday morning we were off again having had breakfast at a small cafe and snatching a wash in the bathroom. Back into England through the West Midlands before finally entering the West Country and parking at Twerton Park Bath, the home at the time of Bristol Rovers. Wednesday morning we were woken again by a lady bringing us cups of coffee and asking if we would like breakfast, the reply was obvious but we also asked if there was somewhere we could wash first and for the second time on the trip we were allowed to use the home dressing room showers. Clean and dressed we walked into the clubhouse to be confronted by the biggest fry up I think I have ever seen. The plates were charger size and every inch of them was covered in food they were enormous. Needless to say it did not take the four of us that long to empty our plates and after a second cup of coffee each we got in the van and headed off. There were a lot of miles to do today and not many clubs to visit as we were heading to Bristol then into Wales to visit Swansea and Cardiff then back into England and on to Devon and Cornwall but they had to be done. By the time we reached Plainmoor the home of Torquay United, it was nearly 10pm they had been involved in an FA Cup 1st Round Replay against at the time non-league Kidderminster Harriers winning 1:0. Torquay's manager at the time was ex Notts player Don O Riordan and we had hoped to be able to watch the game but sadly no. However when we arrived we were invited to the boardroom for a drink and a sandwich and Don took time out to chat to all of us. What a gentleman. We thought about staying the night in Torquay but decided to press on as Thursday we would be venturing into London and needed as much time as possible to drive through there so on we went to Plymouth, then on to Bournemouth before calling it a night in the early hours at Dean Court. As uncomfortable as the bus was we were all so exhausted that we slept longer than normal not waking up until gone 8am on Thursday morning. We obviously needed it. We did our usual trick finding a cafe washing in the toilets and off we went along the South Coast then Gillingham and Southend and by late afternoon we had to face it. Next stop London. We arrived on the outskirts of London just after 6pm and decided to stop for a drink and plan our tactics at The Falcon pub just off the A2 and roughly five miles from The Valley, the home of Charlton Athletic and our first Port of Call. So that's what we did. It was decided Terry would do all the driving and as usual we would ask directions. It had served us pretty well up to now. Refreshed and as ready as we ever would be we set off steadily ticking off the grounds at first until we tried to find Selhurst Park the home of Crystal Palace, no one seemed to give us the right directions and already frayed tempers were at breaking point when we finally found it. In all it took us about six hours to visit the thirteen clubs so with thoughts of home and the end of the challenge we drove on to Adams Park the home of Wycombe Wanderers planning to stay the night, our last, in the bus there. We entered High Wycombe about 2am and saw nobody we could ask for ages and when we finally did find somebody his reply to the question "where is Adams Park please?", "Was hey man its all round you, it's everywhere" Great help. We must have wasted an hour driving round but finally found the ground, parked up and settled down. Friday morning arrived all to soon and after a wash in a cafe we were off on the last leg Colchester to East Anglia across to Cambridge, Peterborough and Leicester before finally the Baseball Ground Derby and last of all Meadow Lane. We were home by 7pm sadly not to a blaze of publicity and media but just our wives and families there to greet us. Sadly not even anybody from Notts County. Oh well we had done it 3680 miles and visited all 132 clubs. Time for bed? Not just yet Loraine informed me that we were wanted at the De Montfort Hall in Leicester to appear on the regional BBC Children In Need show to tell them what we had done and how much money we had raised. It was just short of £5000, in fact £4868, which we were delighted with thank you everybody who helped and supported us along the way. From Leicester we drove to the Wheatsheaf Pub on Ilkeston Road at the top end near Canning Circus. It is no longer there but was Mik's local and the landlady Eunice had put on a celebration party for the four of us and presented us all trophy's. On Saturday October 22nd 1994 a few weeks before we set off we had enjoyed a fund raising night there with Billy Ivory supporting us and Tommy Lawton as guest of Honour. Eventually we got to bed. By now we were used to going to sleep late but Mik, Terry and I were all at Meadow Lane the following afternoon to watch a much needed win 2:0 over West Brom thanks to Phil Turner and Gary Lund and all four of us were at Meadow Lane on Tuesday December 6th 1994 for the game against Tranmere Rovers which Notts won 1:0. We were invited on the pitch at half time to explain what we had done and the winning goal by Paul Devlin was scored just after we had left the pitch. Thank you Notts County for that.

What I didn't realise at the time and as far as I am aware nor did anybody else was that in 1994 when we did this 132 club challenge Notts County were 132 years old. On the 19th March 1995 Notts got to Wembley in the final of the Anglo Italian Cup against Ascoli having lost in the final 1:0 to Brescia the year before. I organised a coach for the day and this time both Daniel and Kimberley went with us! They must have been the difference because Notts won 2:1 taking the lead through Tony Agana in the first half and then once Ascoli had equalised getting the winner through Devon White as half time approached.

The Junior Magpies had been running for nearly 20 years when we finally took advantage of their facilities. At the time the Junior Juniors trained on the Old 5 a side Courts at the back of the Kop on a Friday evening and the older ones on a Monday evening between 6 and 8pm so both Daniel aged nearly eight and Kimberley aged nearly five turned up every Friday evening without fail. The sessions were run by Reg Killick with the support of Alan Higgott and Iris Smith. On Saturday February 8th 1997 Daniel went on his first away trip with Reg and Iris on the coach leaving Meadow Lane at 10am going to Gay Meadow to play Shrewsbury Juniors as well as to watch the game he was only 9 and Loraine like any good mother was a bit worried about him so an hour after they had departed we drove there with Kimberley in the car. You can imagine how surprised Daniel was when he saw us in all honesty I think he had been a bit nervous too and sadly it was not a great game to go to, Notts running out losing 2:1 with Dave Regis scoring just after half time to give Notts the lead. Once we had seen Daniel was okay we let him travel back on the coach and over the months and years to come we all got to know each other very well, parents and children, and shared many away trips by coach.

For her 7th birthday on June 21st 1997 I bought Kimberley the All Yellow shirt with the giant emblem on the front of it and wanted to put a name on the back but what? And what number? I wanted the number "½" as she was so small but couldn't find anywhere that could do it for me so I settled on the name RATBAG and the number 0.5. The shirt was far too large for her and went down remarkably well and to this day people still refer to Kimberley as Ratbag. The 1997/8 season started with a home game against Rochdale and the shirt must have been lucky as Notts ran out 2:1 winners, Mark Robson scoring a penalty right on half time and Matt Redmile getting an 89th minute winner after Rochdale had equalised. Kimberley still has that shirt

On Sunday July 18th 1997 the family, all four of us, found ourselves along with Mik at Canary Wharf on the 24th floor at the LIVE TV studios taking part in the quiz show A Game of Two Scarves presented by Rhodri Williams the former Welsh Rugby Union star. LIVE TV was the cable channel run by Kelvin McKenzie that bought us such quality programmes as the Weather in Norwegian and Topless Darts. Mik and I represented Notts County in a match against Reading who were about three hours late turning up. Two scantily clad models did most of the challenges to earn us points so we had no control over that but there were questions as well about our own club. We came second although I must admit I was mainly to blame getting a couple of Notts questions wrong. After that we played Fulham and sadly we came second again not my best hour. I even suggested that Daniel take my place answering the questions in the second game but he wasn't allowed to because of his age. I must admit I have never met anybody who actually watched our shows so I think we got away with it? Unless you know better? LIVE TV closed on November 5th 1999, amazingly, but has now been reincarnated as Babe Station another quality channel.

After one of the best seasons in Notts County's history on Saturday May 2nd 1998 Rotherham visited Meadow Lane for the final game of the season. Notts had wrapped the title up by the end of March when Mark Robson scored in a 1:0 win at home to Leyton Orient, for which a commemorative limited edition picture was commissioned! I have one of these pictures framed on the wall mainly because both Daniel and I are on it, and before kick-off Notts had only lost five games and accumulated ninety six points. It was a day of total celebration from start to finish and I did my bit, Loraine had sold tickets for the club ever since COUNTY 75 had been launched everything from Golden Goal tickets to raffle tickets and at this time 50/50 tickets half the money taken going to the prize the other half to the club so I decided I would help sell some tickets, but first I dressed in a Black Skirt Fishnet Stockings a Black with White flecked Blouse some silicon boobs Black heeled shoes and a Blonde Wig. Maybe subconsciously I knew I would become Mrs Magpie a couple of seasons later. I placed myself outside the main entrance in front of the gates by the side of the Chestnut Tree and sold Half and Half tickets with the tag line operation to pay for. It went down a storm and I sold all the tickets I had been given and many more, not just to Notts fans but Rotherham fans to. As kick off approached I paid my money in and took my usual place in the Family Stand still in my blouse skirt and heels Notts won 5:2 in front of 12430 with two goals from Gary Jones and one each from Dennis Pearce, Sean Farrell and Phil Robinson a tremendous end to a tremendous season 99 points in the bag and a friendly pitch invasion at the end me still in my finery. When I finally met up with Loraine in the Meadow Club she walked in with Big Sam's training top that he had thrown into the crowd and she was delighted to have it as far as I am aware she still has it.

Eventually the Junior Magpies training was amalgamated into one session on a Monday evening as numbers dropped but remained at Meadow Lane even after the ground was redeveloped. Having read the Sun whilst on a meal break in the NCT canteen in the third week of February 1999 I noticed on the Bizarre Show business page (not a page I often read I must admit) that the then journalist Dominic Mohan (he went on to become Editor of the paper and is currently CEO of entertainment public relations company The Outside Organisation) was putting out an appeal asking if anybody had a copy of the single Diamond Lights, which was released in April 1987 entering the charts at number 30 and reaching a high of number twelve the following week. It stayed in the charts for eight weeks and was sung by Glenn Hoddle and Chris Waddle the then Tottenham Hotspurs and England team mates as Glenn Hoddle on February 2nd 1999 had had his contract terminated as England manager because of controversial things he had said in an interview for The Times newspaper the week before. Mr Mohan wanted to set up a phone line so anybody and everybody could listen to the song. I knew Loraine had a copy so without asking I rang Mr Mohan and told him this and he asked if he could have it. Happily, was my reply and I went on to explain we were Notts County supporters and on Saturday 20th 1999 we were travelling down to Craven Cottage for the game against Fulham and were more than happy to bring it with us if he would meet us. He was delighted and arranged to meet us at The Sun's headquarters at Wapping about 10am and sure enough he was waiting for us when we arrived. He was more than happy to see us and not only took the single from us but gave us a few hundred pounds as a reward. Fabulous. He was then kind enough to lead us to Stamford Bridge as the children wanted to visit and Kimberley wanted a Chelsea replica strip and was good enough to then give us directions to Craven Cottage before he left us. Sadly the day went down hill from there as despite Fulham missing a penalty Notts lost the game 2:1, Gary Owers scoring with less than ten minutes to go when Notts were already two down. Not only that but at half time we were treated to Fulham owner Mohamed Al Fayed and two "minders" walking round the pitch and waving at us, the Notts fans, as well as the home fans.

On Wednesday November 3rd 1999 Notts travelled to play Stoke City at the Britannia Stadium and the Supporters Club ran a juniors coach. At time of kick off Notts were third and Stoke were 5th in the table and whoever won went top but it was still classified as a low category match so there were no police in attendance. Notts took the lead in the 23rd minute when Alex Dyer scored but the rest of the game saw wave after wave of Stoke attacks roared on by most of the 11619 crowd. Darren Ward was inspired and amazingly Notts won 1:0 and returned to the top of the league. We all boarded the coach to head back to Nottingham when it was attacked by yobs with stones and bricks and many windows were smashed the younger children were terrified as were some of the older ones but we couldn't do anything as there were no police around. When all had eventually calmed down Matt Redmile and Nick Fenton came on the bus to see we were all okay and to chat to some of the youngsters. A nice gesture which certainly helped settle them down.

After weeks of planning by me and a lot of help from various people and businesses on Saturday July 22nd 2000 the Junior Magpies arrived at the

Power League Soccer Centre on Thane Road to compete in a 24 hour Football Marathon raising funds for "Wish Upon A Star". Alan Higgott the Junior Magpies co ordinator, who was also the referee for the whole time apart from when he was actually playing a match, split the 33 assembled people and 1 dog (Rags) into two teams of juniors and two teams of older people and parents one team playing for Wish Upon A Star the other team playing for the Junior Magpies but the teams were very interchangeable especially later in the night. As with the best laid plans things started to unravel before the first ball was kicked, it had been agreed that we could use the main pitch at the centre but a corporate match was being played there most of the afternoon so we were given a corner pitch with the understanding we moved later.... We stayed on the same pitch all 24 hours, it had been agreed the bar area could be used as the indoor bedroom for the children but there was an 18th birthday party so it wouldn't be available until the early hours of Sunday and to top it all off there was an Open Day at Boots so Thane Road was full of traffic. Problems overcome and St Johns in place we were all ready and eager to go. It had been arranged that Andy Hughes would come to start the event so a young Evening Post photographer was waiting as the clock ticked towards midday. No sign of Hughsie. The reporter was worried as she had somewhere else to go, Andy appeared at 12:05 he had been stuck in the traffic, pictures were taken and then at 12:08 he got the game going and we were off, 24 hours to go. To start with it was planned that each match would last 20 minutes and I kept score. The first match finished 5:1 to "Wish Upon A Star", the first goal was scored by Matt Wheat. That afternoon Notts County were playing a pre-season friendly at Ilkeston Town so my wife Loraine and one of the other Mum's, Sheena, went bucket in hand to raise more money. They got lost on the way but when they found their way back they had collected £117.03 and Notts had drawn 1:1 with Mark Stallard scoring. Thanks to all who gave money. During the afternoon Radio Nottingham came along to do a few interviews and then just after 6pm Barbara White from Wish Upon A Star appeared with McDonalds Burger and Chips for everybody kindly donated by McDonalds on Castle Marina. Carl at Coca Cola Schweppes had donated Capri Sun, Coca Cola and Vittel Water much to the disappointment of Paul Taylor and his staff at the Power League. By midnight the 20 minute rotation had disappeared and it got to the stage that whoever wanted to play could play and that included the St

Johns Ambulance people. The weather had got worse it was pouring with rain so it became very difficult to encourage the youngsters to come back out on the pitch and play. By 1am we were down to three a side and even I was out there trying my best but as anybody knows I play football very badly and I was getting worried that we would not be able to complete the 24 hours (even Rags had a run on the pitch and proved himself a very able defender, just ask Sheena). Luckily about then two of Alan's work colleagues and two friends appeared, I did my fastest running getting off the pitch and back to the scoring and momentum was restored. By 8am Sunday morning with the breakfast cooking all the children were awake and eager to participate again and we were back to the 20 minute matches and all was plain sailing. By 11am all those who had gone home plus some parents had appeared, as had Barbara White again and for the last hour anybody and everybody joined in. In the last minute Loraine, Iris, Angie (St Johns), Barbara White and Sheena were in one of the goals and all the available footballs (7) were being fired at them by anybody and everybody. The 1144th and final goal was scored by Ryan Eaton. A great way to finish a fun event, as the finish line approached Graham Moran from Notts County Football in the Community came to congratulate us donate £20 and at the final whistle to present certificates, designed by Mike Wyer and medals, donated by me to all those who had taken part. For the record the match finished 572:572 and no it was NOT fixed at all! The scorers were:

JUNIOR MAGPIES:		WISH UPON A STAR:	
Ryan Eaton	120	Marcus Eaton	109
Marcus Eaton	68	Matt Wheat	69
Matt Wheat	54	Tom Wheat	58
Tom Ellis	48	Ryan Eaton	49
James O Dell	38	Daniel Walster	37
Ashley Storey	34	James O Dell	31
John Harvey	29	Rob Smeeton	28
Matt Rimmington	20	Alan Higgott	26
Damien Murphy	19	John Harvey	16
Dan De Quincey	19	Carl Swift	16

Alan Higgott	12 +1 og	Wayne Mullins	16
Alan Page	13	Dan De Quincey	16
Tom Wheat	13	Matt Rimmington	14
Ian Openshaw	12	Mik Wyer	13
Josh Hawkridge	11	Nathan Holmes	2
Daniel Walster	11	Ian Openshaw	10
Carl Swift	10	Sheena Hawkridge	8
Rob Smeeton	9	Ashley Storey	5+2 og
Wayne Mullins	7	Josh Hawkridge	6
Carwin Smith	5	John Wise	5 +1 og
Nathan Holmes	4	Alan Page	5
Kim Walster	4	Damien Murphy	5
John Wise	4	Tony Walster	4
Tony Walster	2	Tom Ellis	3
Jim Auld (St Johns)	2	Kelly Holmes	2
Charlie Smith	1	Carwin Smith	2
Loraine Walster	1	Kim Walster	1
Nick Holmes	1	Geoff Smeeton	1
		Iris Smith	1
		Nick Holmes	1
TOTAL	572	TOTAL	572

One in every five goals was scored by one of the Twins either Marcus or Ryan Eaton, Marcus (they had just turned 14) getting the bragging rights scoring 177 to his brothers 169. Many many thanks to all who took part from Robin Smith, who had just turned 5, to Iris Smith who was a bit older and everybody in between. What a fabulous 24 hours but NEVER AGAIN. Finally football training did move firstly to Victoria Embankment where we played on a Monday night throughout the summer but as Autumn approached we were having to use the headlights of the few cars there to light the pitch so it was time for a move again, this time to the all weather pitches at Carlton Forum. Still on a Monday evening, rain or shine, the children turned up along with the same few parents for a two hour session.

The Supporters Club and Junior Magpies ran a coach to Bournemouth on Tuesday October 24th 2000 as it was half term, leaving Meadow Lane at 9am and enabling us to spend the day at the seaside before watching the match later. There were 40 plus children and half a dozen adults onboard including myself, Mik, Sheena, Loraine, (who had been dared along with Sheena to play beach volleyball in their bikinis. But not by me I hasten to add), Daniel, Kimberley and Iris the Supporters Club and Junior Magpies Coordinator. The journey was very uneventful and after a thirty minute obligatory stop at Cherwell Valley services we arrived at Dean Court about 1:30pm. The coach parked up in the car park outside the ground and we all got off and headed off for the beach. It was a walk of roughly two miles in a bracing breeze, the ladies leading the way and me (as one of only two men in the party) bringing up the rear making sure we all kept together. Once on the seafront the wind was blowing more severely and the tide was well in. To every ones amazement, not least because it was near the end of October, Loraine and Sheena did then strip down to their bikini tops and shorts and to a huge round of applause and much cheering they started playing beach volleyball, barmy or what? But I couldn't fault them. Slowly the children joined in ignoring the fact they were getting wet and neglecting to realise there was only one towel between them. When the fun was over the problem was how to dry everybody off with only that towel. The solution was fairly simple, use the hand dryers in the nearby public toilets. It took a while but was very effective. Dried and dressed again we headed for the amusement arcades, no seaside visit is complete without a visit of this kind. A good hour passed and by then thoughts turned to finding something to eat and also heading back towards Dean Court as it was getting colder and dusk was setting in. By now I was the only male, Mik had gone off on his own hours before but like earlier I bought up the rear and off we went. We set off in what we thought was the right direction but we soon realised as it got darker we were lost and for some reason, that I still do not understand to this day this was my fault, as I was at the rear. On we plodded along the Christchurch Road and just after 5pm we came across a fish and chip shop that was just opening. We had found tea! You should have seen the look on the bemused shopkeepers face when 40 plus children and a couple of adults entered her shop asking for fish and chips, pie and chips, anything and chips. I honestly have no idea but I would not mind betting that no sooner had we all walked away than the shop shut again, she cannot have had a Tuesday teatime as busy as that for a long time, if ever. Everybody kept asking me what I wanted and I kept saying "nothing" not because I wasn't hungry but because I knew that there would be plenty left over when the children had eaten what they wanted and I could then have my choice. That is exactly what happened and I had a really good meal. Now the task of getting to the ground before kick-off but that was easily solved. It was dark now and consequently the floodlights were on and we just headed towards them getting there just after 6:30 having had so far a really great day. So to the game which being polite was less than exciting and with five minutes to go looked destined to be scoreless. Then shock, in the 85th minute Mark Stallard scored from the penalty spot. He raced over to the Notts fans to celebrate and incurred an FA charge we found out later. As it happened that was the winning goal so maybe the charge was worth it.

Christmas approached it got colder but still we all turned up at Carlton Forum on a Monday evening. The Junior Supporters Club ran a coach to the New Den on Saturday December 30th 2000. The Junior Magpies at this stage regularly played matches against the junior supporters of the team Notts County were playing, today Millwall and they would come to play the juniors in Nottingham in the reverse fixture. As it was the last away trip of the year it was also decided it would be the party bus. All the adults bought food mainly crisps and nibbles but sandwiches and fizzy drinks as well and the coach was decorated with streamers and ribbons. It was at 8am in my brand new "Christmas present" a replica home shirt, I boarded the 59 seater double decker coach, a luxury as we usually only had normal coaches not ones with an upstairs, along with roughly forty Juniors aged from ten to seventeen and ten other adults. Myself and Alan Higgott were the only adult males travelling. We were due at the New Den for midday and not only were we going to play football but they were going to feed us. The journey was uneventful for the most part. The quiz was completed and the raffle and the sweepstake to pick a shirt number based on the squad numbers in the match day programme when we got there to win money. If that player scored for whichever team the prize divided by however many goalscorers there were. If none the people who picked the goalkeepers won half each. We had the obligatory stop at Toddington services about 9:45am for half an hour and the majority of the children had a bit of a kick about in the car park, although some bought burgers irrespective of the fact they were playing football shortly and they were also getting burgers for lunch. Back on the coach we were doing very well for time. We got to the end of the M1 at Brent Cross turned off the motorway up the slip road to the North Circular and then, the coach "died" and stopped on the slip road with Brent Cross Shopping Centre to one side and the North Circular just yards in front of us. A charming place that we were to get to know well in the next couple of hours. As you do in these situations not realising how serious things are everybody cheered and started ribbing the driver. It was 11:45ish by now so we still had time to get going again and get to the ground but the coach refused to start no matter what the driver did. We were stranded on the slip road with the door opening onto the moving traffic, not the pavement. The driver rang his bosses explaining his situation and was told a replacement coach would be dispatched but Nottingham was three hours away and time was ticking. What else could we do? Time ticked on, midday came and went, 1pm came and went and as the North Circular got busier and busier so did the slip road, some impatient people even showing their ignorance as they hooted at the coach as they passed. We were not there for the fun of it when all said and done. We accepted we would not get there early enough to play the juniors now the question was would we see the match? Just after 2:30 pm a new coach appeared on the North Circular, great, at last but how were we going to get to it? It was decided the best thing to do was to reverse the new coach down the slip road. Who decided this I have no idea? But that meant somebody had to walk up the slip road, walk out into the traffic on the North Circular and stop all three lanes. I was chosen to do that or asked to anyway. So dressed in my new shirt I walked up the slip road and stepped out into the traffic, turned my back on the oncoming traffic and spread my arms wide with my eyes tightly shut. Initially there was nothing but the sound of car horns and cars continuing to fly past me but amazingly after a few minutes the traffic slowed and eventually stopped. Thank goodness for that. The replacement coach then reversed down the slip road and the adults formed a wall as best as they could from one coach door to the other enabling the children to board the new coach as safely as possible. I was called to come and join them as we were ready to go. Thank goodness. I jumped on the coach and the driver told me to sit in the courier seat at the front and handed me his mobile phone saying talk to Tower Bridge Police tell them we are mobile again. They are going to give us an escort to the ground. Sure enough within minutes, two police cars with lights and sirens on appeared and led us the last few miles to the ground. A police escort to Millwall! That must be a first? We arrived at 3:05 and just as we were getting out there was a cheer, a goal? Who for? Who knew? We didn't but we were to find out Andy Hughes had just put us in front. Millwall still insisted on giving us burgers and chips as we got in the ground, they were disgusting, and cold, but a kind gesture. By 15:15 we were all in the ground just as Millwall equalised, no need to worry even though we only saw a 2:1 win Notts ran out 3:2 winners with another goal from Andy Hughes and a last minute winner from Gary Owers.

Pete Lawson had volunteered to go to Pride Park Derby on Friday October 6th 2000 as a mascot to represent Notts County in the Under 21 International between England and Germany. It finished 1:1 with Titus Bramble scoring to give England the lead. Pete hated the costume, it was nothing more than a black bin liner with a head and he came back with tales of how he was abused spat on pulled about and generally ridiculed and he hated the whole experience so the Supporters Club decided to invest in real costumes. They were looking for two volunteers to wear the costumes and having volunteered I got my dream job as one of either Mr or Mrs Magpie depending who else volunteered to do the job. It turned out the other volunteer was Sheena, whose son Josh was in the Junior Magpies as well and was a good friend of mine. The costumes when we first saw them were huge very cumbersome and the only thing to keep your head secure was a bicycle helmet inside the head but that did not make much difference when it came to seeing where you were going, especially when running, and in time we realised you could see and not breath or breath and not see. The costumes were picked up from a shop in Newark on Monday January 15th 2001 and Sheena and I made our debut the following Saturday January 20th at home to Rotherham and a great start to the mascots life, Notts running out 4:1 winners having trailed 1:0 at half time. Obviously Mr and Mrs Magpie take all the credit for their half time performance that inspired Anders Jacobsen to equalise and Richard Liburd to put us ahead on the hour. Andy

Hughes then scored and Mark Stallard sealed it. So logic would dictate I would be Mr Magpie & Sheena Mrs Magpie. Where was the fun in that? We were having none of it so I became Mrs Magpie which confused many referees and opposing captains over the years and I played the role for over 10 seasons finishing with more husbands than Joan Collins. We were both extremely nervous that first game but soon relaxed and enjoyed ourselves knowing at the time very few people knew who we were and we could do anything we wanted, the dafter the better, on the pitch.

On Saturday September 9th 2000, Notts had entertained Bristol Rovers in what turned out to be a very controversial ill-tempered game. Bristol Rovers took the lead on the hour and from then on wasted as much time as possible with players dropping to the floor whenever they could. By the 88th minute the fans had seen enough and when another Rovers player did his "dying swan" act in front of Z block in the County Road Stand they vociferously suggested to Craig Ramage that he didn't throw the ball back (a gentleman's agreement in football but not law). Instead Ramage threw the ball to Richard Liburd who crossed for Mark Stallard to equalise and all hell broke out. There was a twenty two man brawl after Marcus Bignot viciously took out Ramages' legs and having retaliated Ramage got sent off. Bignot got a yellow amazingly, Jocky Scott the Notts manager kept all the players on the pitch at the end of the game to avoid any more possible confrontations in the tunnel and Bristol Rovers manager Ian Holloway demanded the match be replayed which would have set a major precedent. The Rovers manager had to be ordered onto the team coach by the police as things didn't calm down throughout the evening until they left. Fast forward five months and Mrs Magpies appearance on Saturday 10th February 2001 at The Memorial Ground Bristol. Maybe I shouldn't have gone in costume? Sheena certainly didn't so I went alone, I do not know but needless to say it was the most hostile reception I have ever had anywhere. I honestly think some of the Bristol Rovers supporters would have hurt me if I had got close enough and the language throughout the game was enough to make a coal miner blush. Luckily Notts came away with a draw 0:0 this time and by the end of the season Bristol Rovers were relegated by one point. If only Stallard hadn't scored they would have stayed up, shame. The costumes were big and bulky as already stated and as time went by I learnt it was sensible to wear as little as possible underneath as you got so warm even in the middle of winter. As you can imagine keeping them clean fresh and laundered was a priority.

On Sunday April 1st 2001 we were invited to our first mascot event at Gay Meadow to play a mascot football match in front of a paying audience. The crowd on the day was 2163 I am told and 48 mascots were in attendance. Mascots from various clubs appeared from Blackpool to Plymouth Bradford to Queens Park Rangers and many clubs in between. As it was our first such event we arrived very early with our respective families but were soon put at our ease by the friendly people at Gay Meadow. As the morning progressed more and more mascots appeared from all over the country, people I was to get to know really well over the next decade both in costume and out. I am still friends with many of them. The pre match entertainment included a display from the Tricky Tykes display team and also the Shrewsbury Town FC cheerleaders then it was our turn. It finished up about twenty four a side anything goes with a fabulous referee called Maelor Owen, a local Shropshire FA official for over 20 years, who joined in the spirit of things but like many of the mascot events over the years most of the time it appeared he had no control on what was going on at all. The crowd loved it as did I and I was hooked it was tremendous fun although as it was quite warm and sunny I was soon flagging. It is amazing how big a full size football pitch is when you in a bulky costume and the sun is shining, but water was in plentiful supply and it was a great laugh with mascots regularly leaving the pitch to interact with the crowd. A brief review of the match report reads "the game was full of fun and laughter with plenty to enjoy. The game was notable for two hat tricks scored by Cyril the Swan from Swansea and Alex the Greek from Exeter City. Cyril was the first mascot sent off to be followed by Alex the Greek and Benny Buck from Telford. The final score was 8:2 with the two hat tricks, Super Saint from Southampton and Bloomfield Bear from Blackpool scoring at one end Lenny City Gent from Bradford City and Yorkie from York City scoring at the other end, but the score was irrelevant all the mascots did their best to entertain the crowd and everyone was a winner. At the end of the game all the mascots were presented with medals and a lovely plaque which still adorns my cabinet in the front room.

A few times each season the costumes were dry cleaned and at the end of every season they were sent to a National chain of dry cleaners for a "deep clean". To that end on Monday May 7th 2001, two days after our final game of the season, a 2:1 win at home to Oxford United with goals by David Joseph and Mark Stallard winning it, Notts having fallen behind and Oxford finishing bottom of the league and dropping into Non-League football which finished off a fair season with Notts finishing 8th, I duly took the costumes minus their shirts, which Loraine always washed, to be cleaned knowing they would not be needed for a couple of months, allowing plenty of time for them to be thoroughly cleaned ready for the next season. I was told they would be ready in six to eight weeks, perfect. However as usual things did not work entirely to plan. The week after the costumes were handed over the mascots were invited to London Weekend Television to appear live at the end of Ant and Dec's television show Slap Bang on Saturday 16th June 2001 (only five weeks away). We had to be at the television studios as near midday as we could although the show was not broadcast live until later in the evening about 5:30pm for an hour. Iris was also invited to sit in the audience and watch the show so I went back to the dry cleaners to explain the situation and see what they could do to get the costumes ready. I was told they would be ready by the 8th of June, so plenty of time. Back I went on June 8th to be informed that the costumes had "gone missing" and nobody knew where they were, now what? Over the next few days I went in every day to see what was happening and finally on June 15th I was informed the costumes were in Hemel Hempstead. They offered to get them back to Nottingham by courier, an offer that I declined, instead it was agreed that we would call in on our way down to London and pick them up to save any further problems. I was told the warehouse at the Industrial Estate we were heading to in Hemel Hempstead opened at 9am on a Saturday so it would fit our timetable on our way to London. Saturday dawned dry and overcast but got very warm later. The mascot shirts were laid on the bed by Loraine. I got myself ready in my White Notts away shirt (this seasons 3rd strip) and by 7am I was off to pick Iris up from Bulwell before picking Sheena up from Draycott, she was wearing the Tangerine and Black Notts away shirt, (the 2nd strip) and heading down the M1 towards London. We arrived at Hemel Hempstead just after 9am, found our way to the Industrial Estate where we hoped to find the costumes and on finding the building we wanted we found it was locked and the shutters were down, time to panic. Thankfully not as a couple of minutes later a very disinterested lady appeared without a rush in her she slowly went about opening the building. So far so good but as we entered she disappeared out the back with no explanation coming back a few minutes later with a cup of coffee, only the one but that did not really matter all we wanted were the costumes. Finally she turned to us and said "yes?" nothing more, quickly I tried to explain the situation but before I had finished she had disappeared out the back again and came back with the costumes saying "thank god they are gone at last bloody things". Without a word of thanks I grabbed the costumes and we walked out the office I did however shout "have a nice day" as we left. I didn't wait for her reply. By 9:15am the costumes were back in our possession at last and safely in the back of the car, so on we drove. We were in good time to get to the studios for midday so when we arrived at Barnet we found a very smart Harvester and went in for breakfast and a cup of coffee. It was about this moment that disaster struck again! It suddenly dawned on me the mascot shirts were still lying freshly laundered on my bed at home. What could we do? We did not have time to drive back and fetch them. I dare not tell Iris, what a mess! There was nothing else for it but to get to the studios and try and think of something. We arrived safely Iris was whisked away even though the show was not being broadcast for more than five hours and we were shown into a room with our fellow mascots. About sixty of them had or did turn up and it was good as usual to catch up with old friends. By midday we had been moved to an area behind the studio, part indoors part outdoors where all the dressing rooms were and then we sat or stood chatting and waiting for whatever happened next. This gave me time to confess to Sheena and see what she could think of? Once she had calmed down and stopped laughing we set about thinking of a solution. Mid-afternoon we were called on stage to do a rehearsal and to be told what we could and could not do. We were all entering the stage at the end of the show some from the left wing some the right and some from the back of the stage. We were entering from the back of the stage as the credits were being played and were told where to stand, what to do and no getting in the way of Ant and Dec or the other Celebrities, Robbie Williams amongst them. No misbehaving, no bad language not that any could be heard inside the costumes and it was stressed no scarves. Just then I had a flash of inspiration. Sheena and I cannot be described as "stick thin" more cuddly than that so why not use the shirts we were wearing on the costumes. They would fit with a bit of a struggle and we had plenty of time to get them on as we were basically all sitting around doing nothing and I also had a Notts scarf which I would take on stage with me. We had been told not to but what could they do? With hold our fee I guess but as it was the end of the show a chance worth taking. So that is what we did and nobody ever knew the difference and if you really want to see it there is a clip on "You Tube" posted by Freddy the Fox. Even if I say so myself Mr and Mrs Magpie stand out quite nicely amongst the crowd of mascots and me holding the scarf up makes it look even better.

Notts County had a pre-season tour of Scotland from Thursday July 26th 2001 until Monday July 30th 2001 taking in 3 games against Stirling Albion Partick, Thistle and East Fife so when the school summer holidays started on Wednesday July 25th Loraine, Kimberley and I were parked at Arnold Hill School waiting for Daniel to finish, the car all loaded up for a trip North of the border. Our plan was? Well we didn't actually have a plan as we set off just get as far North as we could and then decide where to go and watch a pre-season game that night. On the journey we finally decided is was going to be either Queen of the South at home to Darlington or preferably Queens Park at home to Ayr United. I fancied going to Hampden Park. We only got as far as Dumfries before time beat us, Queen of the South versus Darlington it would be then. We located the ground, Palmerston Park, by 6:35ish and from there we drove round looking for somewhere to stay the night. Within 10 minutes we had found a bed and breakfast 2 streets from the ground and they had vacancies. All was falling into place nicely. We checked in washed changed and were walking to the ground by 7:20. There were a couple of hundred people in the ground by kick off, including from what we could see 3 Darlington supporters and us 4 Notts County supporters. It was a typical early pre-season game all huff puff and rush with very little skilful football being played by either side. In the end Darlington ran out easy 3:0 winners. For the record at Hampden Park, Ayr United won 2:0. On the walk back to our digs we found a fish and chip shop with tables and chairs went inside and had tea. Scotch Egg, Beans and Chips for me, it is not often chip shops serve Scotch Eggs, certainly not South of the Border, then back to the bed and breakfast and bed. Friday morning after a hearty breakfast we were on our way to Stirling for the first Notts County game against Stirling Albion at the Forthbank Stadium with a capacity of 3808. We had already booked a room in a Premier Inn within walking distance of the ground, as had many other Notts fans, so having checked in and unpacked we went for a walk round the city and to do a bit of sightseeing. We found our way to the castle and a pub called the City Walls where we went in and had something to eat along with other Notts fans. We then sat out in the sunshine enjoying a drink before walking back to the stadium for the match. To say the first half was slow paced was an understatement, it was no more than a training session but having fallen behind to a goal from Neil Bennett after 25 minutes by half time Notts were 3:1 up with goals from Darren Caskey Marcel Cas, Danny Allsopp and Ian Hamilton finished things off in the second half with a screamer from distance to make the final score Notts County 4:1 Stirling Albion in front of a good sized crowd, the majority of which had travelled from Nottingham. Back to the hotel and a drink in the bar before heading upstairs to bed. Friday was spent sightseeing again around Stirling and then on Saturday morning we drove to Glasgow for the second match against Partick Thistle. Partick is in the dock area of Glasgow and is with the greatest of respect rather rough. As we approached there were burnt out cars, old televisions and fridges in the front gardens and the children were running around barefoot and with their backsides hanging outside their trousers. We found a McDonald's near the ground and the 4 of us in our Notts shirts went in for lunch. As we entered the whole place went silent and every eye turned towards us, nice. We found a table I fetched the food and before we left Daniel needed the toilet. Within seconds of him going inside three or four youngsters followed so I had to go and make sure he was okay which he was. On to the stadium and by kick off there were roughly 1500 people inside. Notts put in an awful display the only shining light being Tony Hackworths goal in the first half. If it hadn't been for Stuart Garden in goal they could and should probably have lost. It was the first day of the Scottish Premier League season and Celtic the defending champions were kicking off against St Johnstone at Parkhead at 5:35pm, I would have loved to have gone as a few Notts fans did but sadly we were heading home as Loraine and I both had work on Monday. Celtic won 3:0 Johan Mjalby scoring before half time and Paul Lambert adding 2 more after the break. For the record Notts finished their tour on Monday

30th at the Bayview Stadium against East Fife and by all accounts we missed the best match of the three, Notts winning 6:1 with 2 own goals from John Ovenstone and Paul Mortimer and a brace from Tony Hackworth putting them 4:0 ahead at half time. Ian Hamilton and Nick Fenton added two more before a consolation goal from Paul Mortimer.

On Tuesday 18th September 2001 we decided to travel as a family to Prenton Park to watch Notts take on Tranmere Rovers. It was the day before my 37th birthday. We drove up and parked we found ourselves in the away end, as we all know loving named the cowshed, and prepared for the match. Tranmere took an early lead but by half time Notts were 2:1 in front with goals from Darren Caskey and Marcel Cas. Sadly that was as good as it got for Notts, in the second half Tranmere scored three times without reply eventually running out 4:2 winners. So to the journey home. Down the M6 I have no idea if it was because I was tired or Loraine as navigator was tired or we both were but we went sailing past junction 15 heading south. Never mind we would have to get off at junction 14. I didn't realise how far away it was roughly eleven miles so I made sure we didn't miss it and headed off up the A34 back to Stoke and home following a taxi then to finish the evening off we both got flashed by a speed camera, the first time I had ever had any points on my licence. It was an awful end to a rotten early birthday but I should have known better I was born on a Saturday in the football season so Notts surely played not at all they played on the Friday night getting a 0:0 draw at Belle Vue Doncaster. I have been around since 1964 and in that time Notts have played on my actual birthday September 19th nine times, winning none, drawing one and losing the rest including a 6:1 hiding at Meadow Lane on Tuesday 19th September 1972 at the hands of Charlton Athletic, with Les Bradd scoring a late consolation goal, and a 6:0 hiding at The Den on Saturday 19th September 1992. Guess I am just lucky? The grim record so far reads played 9 won 0 drawn 1 and lost 8 Scored 5 conceded 24. Anybody else have a Lucky birth date?

Saturday October 27th 2001 saw a rather unusual straightforward mascot assignment. Notts County were away against Bournemouth and the Supporters Club were as usual running a bus and Mr and Mrs Magpie were invited to attend. Nothing unusual about that I know but at the time Bournemouth were playing their home games at the Avenue Stadium Dorchester as Dean Court was being renovated. The coach driver found the place but there was so much normal Saturday shopping traffic it was nearly 2:50pm when we finally parked up, but it didn't stop me grabbing the costumes and getting changed. Alone again that day sadly and doing my bit on the pitch. It seemed to inspire the players because by the 25th minute Notts were two up with goals from Tony Hackworth and Danny Allsopp but then the referee took centre stage and by half time he had awarded Bournemouth two penalties, the second one on the stroke of half time to put Bournemouth 3:2 ahead at the break and booked three Notts players. Notts had four more players booked in the second half and Simon Grayson sent off even though the card was later rescinded. In the meantime Bournemouth had one player booked and scored a fourth goal running out 4:2 winners. Because of the inaccessibility of the stadium, positioned right next to a superstore, it was a nightmare leaving the ground as well and while waiting to exit the car park we listened to the FA Cup first round draw. A trip to the Abbey Stadium Cambridge bought a great end to a different sort of a day.

On a frosty misty Thursday evening the 15th November 2001 Mr and Mrs Magpie arrived at Nottingham Greyhound Stadium. This evening there was a different husband for me as Sheena was unavailable, so Tony a work colleague took her place at Colwick to take part in the Pudsey Bear Stakes, running the finishing straight of the Greyhound Track. Luckily, we did not have to use the Starting Gates as most of us would never have got out again out of costume never mind in them. There was a turn out of local mascots as I said Mr and Mrs Magpie were there as was Sherwood the Bear from across the Trent, Rammie from Derby, Nice Bear from The Arena, Paws representing Nottingham Panthers Ice Hockey team, Welford the Tiger from Leicester Tigers as well as Pudsey himself. They found us a little box room to change in which did not leave much room for the eight of us but we certainly got to know each other a little better. At the designated time we were called outside and paraded in the centre of the ring in front of the crowd before being led to our starting position at the start of the final straight. We were all assembled, some taking the run seriously and some playing to the crowd. I was torn. I had never won any mascot race always being a few pounds overweight and this race was no exception the problem being as stated previously the mascot costumes always hampered things but in a fair race I must admit I fancied my chances. We were called together Under Starters Orders and we were off no rabbit to chase just a sprint down the home straight. The next 30 to 40 seconds were a blur I gave it everything I had and more besides and crossed the line in 2nd place, I was absolutely delighted and the trophy still sits permanently on display in my dining room. I was beaten by Rammie with Mr Magpie (Tony) coming 3rd and Sherwood? he may be still running! As far as I know even Pudsey beat him or maybe he won the next race he was that slow, but all credit to everybody it was a great fun night and the rumours of skull duggery by the winner, well all I can say is, I honestly have no idea but hope it was a fair race. Loraine and the children and Iris were as happy as me with a 2nd placed finish and were totally as disbelieving as me that I had managed to get that close to the front, Rammie only just beat me in the end. Another trophy to add to my collection and I am as proud of this one as all the others.

On Saturday March 30th 2002 the Queen Mother passed away at the age of 101 on Easter Monday April 1st Notts County played QPR at Loftus Road and Mrs Magpie attended sadly alone again. I as usual was given a small box room to change in and pre game I went out with Jude the Cat the QPR mascot and entertained the supporters and as the match started I changed and was allowed to watch the first half in an Executive Box. A first half that started brilliantly, Paul Hefferenan and Ian Barraclough putting Notts 2 up within 35 minutes, that was as good as it got, the referee found a few minutes extra time at the end of the half and in that time QPR scored. Half time 2:1, I was back in costume and missed the goal. After having been out on the pitch at half time I changed into my Notts shirt and went to join the other Notts supporters. Usually at the away end at Loftus Road supporters are put in the top tier of a two tier stand but today, we were in the lower tier, so having changed I carried the costumes along the upper tier to the far side of the ground then took the stairs down to the lower tier where I found a young steward who started by asking me "are you a Notts County fan?" I said yes I was, thinking it was fairly obvious he then said "are you from Nottingham?", again I thought it was fairly obvious but acknowledged the fact. He then went on to say "shame about the Queen Mother but at least

she is there now sat on God's right hand side looking down on us". I have
to admit I was not expecting that and excusing myself I put the costumes
down and joined the fans in time to see QPR score twice more and win 3:2.
At the end of the game I picked the costumes up. They were at the time
transported in a double quilt cover and walked out the ground to the coach
when one London Wag shouted "what you got in there?" My reply of "the
body of the last idiot who asked that question" shut him up straight away.

On Sunday March 17th 2002, Lenny the City Gent from Bradford City
invited me (and Mr Magpie who wasn't available) and a few other mascots,
(Captain Blade from Sheffield United Billy Brewer from Burton Albion
Benny the Buck from Telford Poacher the Imp from Lincoln Chaddy the
Owl from Oldham Whaddney from Cheltenham and Yorkie from York
City) the regular few, to his Great Nephew Bradley Middlecoops 8th birthday
party at the Manor Complex in Mansfield. We had a football match in the
gym the children versus the mascots (it has to be said Captain Blade is a
half decent goalkeeper in costume) and then played games throughout the
afternoon. Lenny bought a lot of magic tricks off Harry Corbett (born and
bred in Bradford and his uncle was Harry Ramsden) so he entertained all
of us with some of those as well as making animals out of balloons. A great
time was had by all.

Sunday June 9th 2002 must have been one of the wettest days on record as
Tony and I travelled to the Reebok Stadium for an Open Day, Bolton were
attempting to break the record for the largest group of mascots in one place.
Again we were going to play a match and the pre match entertainment was
provided by a school children's 5 a side tournament as well as displays by
the Sea Cadets and the National Canine Defence League. There was also
a competition to find the First Bus Driver of the Year although Tony and
I who were both bus drivers in Nottingham were not allowed to take part.
Then the match. The mascots were announced one by one as they entered
the pitch and by the time it was all sorted there were 32 football mascots
from Gilbert Gull from Torquay to Panda Monium and Chaos from Ayr
United, as well as 22 other mascots from Paws from Nottingham Panthers
to Ernie Eagle from the Ayr Scottish Eagles Ice Hockey Club in a group of
54 mascots. A World Record and a place in the Guinness Book of Records

for all of us. The match was played in torrential rain with John McGinlay the former Bolton player, as the referee. It was a farce but goals kept being scored although the best the Magpies did was for Mr Magpie Tony to get in a scuffle with the Charlton Athletic mascot Floyd on the touchline which resulted in them both rolling around in the mud and rain water. The match finished 6:5 but as usual everybody was given a medal. The costumes were at least three times their normal weight by the time we had finished but within the fortnight they were in A1 shape again.

Hugging, no holding back, totally accepting, entirely non-judgemental, all enveloping, wonderfully warm, emotionally healing, calming and loving. This was Slimming World's definition of a hug before the Guinness World Record attempt in Nottingham. Organised on behalf of the charity Sargent Cancer Care for Children and Slimming World BBC Radio Nottingham presenter Mike Smith lent his weight to a Nottingham attempt to get into the Guinness Book of Records by holding the World's Biggest Hug. He was hoping to attract over 3000 people to the event launching the search live on the radio on Saturday 25th May 2002. Shane Ritchie was also throwing his weight behind the attempt. Those taking part had to pledge £5 to the charity a small price to pay and Tony and I Mr and Mrs Magpie were invited and were more than happy to attend. The previous record was set in Canada on 14th February 2001 and the record was 1802 people or it was but in the days before our attempt the Canadian record was beaten by the Rocori Area Schools in Minnesota who had 2903 people hugging that made things harder. The record breaking attempt was held at Harvey Hadden Stadium on Sunday June 23rd 2002. The day was gloriously sunny as Mr and Mrs Magpie arrived at the Stadium not only was there going to be a record attempt but it was also a fun day with stalls, entertainment live music and amusements. As usually happened at these events the mascots found themselves in goal and much to everyone's delight saved hardly anything, not because the shots were that good but as I have explained in the costumes you could either see and not breathe or breathe and not see and on such a warm afternoon we chose to breathe. There were plenty of people there maybe we could break the record? The time for the record attempt arrived and we were all called to the playing field inside the running track we formed a circle standing on the field Mr and Mrs Magpie were placed in different parts of the circle with the running track behind us and spread wider as more people joined in. It was a bit more formal than most hugs it had to be done in a certain arrangement and the hugging had to be done in a certain way to satisfy the adjudicators from the Guinness Book of Records, who were above us in a helicopter I was informed later, as I couldn't see or hear them. Not only did we have to hug in a certain way but once set we had to stand still long enough for the adjudicators to confirm it was being done correctly and was in fact a record. It was and a group of 3242 of us found ourselves in the Record Books. I still have my certificate to prove it although the records has been beaten many times since that day.

The Mascot Grand National has been held every year since 1999 at Huntingdon Racecourse Sheena and I attending our first race in 2001. A huge event it grew bigger year upon year but eventually became too big and tarnished by professional athletes in the costumes. It started just for football mascots but business and charity mascots soon entered. Mr and Mrs Magpie never had any chance of winning as the costumes are so big and bulky, as are the people inside, but it was always a great day. The race is over the last furlong (660 feet or an eighth of a mile) of the racecourse and to make it easier there are little solid wooden hurdles we have to jump. They are solid so impossible to just run through them. The entrance fee for the race each year was always as much as the mascots could raise and this was donated to charity. A lot of mascots got there clubs to give them the money, this never once crossed my mind I was just so proud to represent Notts County in front of the National media and it was such good fun meeting old friends year after year and having a laugh. In 2002 it was suggested we make an attempt to get in the Guinness Book of Records with the largest Mascot Gathering (and trying to beat the record set at Bolton three months earlier.) The race was scheduled for Sunday 29th September. Every Mascot at every football club in the country was invited and for the one and only time we were offered rooms at the local Marriott Hotel at a discounted rate for bed and breakfast. We stayed there on the Saturday night and, for those that wanted it, the Sunday night as well. Notts were playing Cheltenham at Whadden Road on the Saturday so Tony and I attended with the Loraine, Daniel and Kimberley. Tony could not spend the weekend but was travelling to Huntingdon on the Sunday for the race. As usual we went on the pitch before the game and at half time and by the time we had changed and got back to the Notts fans we had missed three Notts goals, two at the start of the first half, one after half time, so we saw a 1:1 draw with Mark Stallard's second goal Notts actually won 4.1 with two goals from both Mark Stallard and Danny Allsopp. After the game having said goodbye to (Tony) Magpie we drove to the hotel arriving there about 7pm. When we checked in a crowd of mascots were already there. We were allocated our room and Daniel and Kimberley were delighted to find there was a Swimming Pool, a Gym and a Sauna. Loraine who had packed swimming costumes and I already knew, guess we forgot to tell them. After a fun hour we decided to find something to eat. Asking some of the other mascots we were told there was either a chip shop or a pizzeria locally so fish and chips it was then time for a sociable drink with a few old friends. There were between 20 and 30 mascots staying at the hotel from Pilgrim Pete of Plymouth to City Gent of Bradford and all points in between. A sociable drink turned into a couple more and a couple more after that and most of us finally headed to our rooms in the early hours of Sunday morning. Some never made it to bed. After a few hours sleep it was breakfast time. Looking around the Dining Room maybe I stood a chance this year? Some of the mascots looked worse than I felt. Loraine drove us to the racecourse where Mr Magpie was already waiting. We changed as did all the mascots and made our way to the parade ring where all the pre-race photographs and the group photographs were being taken. First of all we paraded around the ring a few times with plenty of us larking around and working off the sore heads then as it was a Guinness World Record attempt, we all joined together for a group photograph. Also present was Catalina Guirado, a 28 year old television presenter who was representing the race sponsors and was awarding the prizes at the end of the race. I was kind enough to let her sit on my knee during the photo shoot which went on for an age, at least 35 to 40 minutes and all this time with her sat on my knee with nobody knowing. Even the pictures do not reveal anything, well us ladies have to stick together and I must admit I enjoyed it. When the formalities were finally over I managed to catch a word with her and cheekily suggested as I had no chance of winning the race that for my kindness I would like to win something else? She suggested "Ugliest Mascot" I jumped at the chance, so onto the racecourse we went all 94 of us lined up and the race started. Several mascots flew down the course, various others including me had such large costumes they could do little more than walk. As we progressed down the course there were more and more discarded bits of mascot costume from big feet to gloves and the stragglers had not reached the second hurdle when Chaddy the Owl the Oldham Athletic mascot crossed the finishing line, but then again his costume was no more than a head and a figure hugging fur suit. As we continued the little jumps to me seemed four feet tall and by the end it was getting hard to even climb over them but finally I crossed the line to a bit of a commotion. Lenny the Lion the Shrewsbury Town mascot had not stopped when he crossed the finishing line and was running a full circuit of the course one mile 3 furlongs much to the annoyance of the organisers, as there were still horse races to be run but the crowd loved it and our main aim was to entertain. So when Lenny finally got back I was presented with a trophy for taking part and a trophy as the Ugliest Mascot and as far as I am aware that particular prize has never been awarded since so Mrs Magpie was in 2002 and still is the "Ugliest Mascot" and I have the trophy to prove it. The following week the Evening Post ran an article asking "is this Britain's Ugliest Mascot?" with a picture of me in my costume but with the head off, charming. Sadly the write up that accompanied the picture didn't do me any justice at all. It read "The Magpies have plundered their first piece of silverware of the season but it has left one man spitting feathers. Mrs Magpie aka Tony Walster is in a flap after being voted the ugliest football mascot in Britain. First he was gutted to finish way down the pecking order after coming 68th in the annual Mascot Grand National at Huntingdon racecourse on Sunday. Mr Magpie aka Wendy Wolf (the name of the female Wolves mascot) meanwhile finished even further back in 71st place. Then Mrs Magpie suffered a further devastating blow as the other racers voted her ugliest of all the mascots (not correct it was awarded by Catalina Guirado) Tony thought Mrs Magpie had been hard done by (I didn't I was and still am absolutely delighted)". I got stick at work for weeks about that one but I was and all these years later still am delighted with the award and the fact that for the third time in as many months Mr and Mrs Magpie Tony and I and Notts County, if not in name were in the Guinness Book of Records as it was confirmed that we had set a record for the largest amount of mascots in one place needless to say broken many times since then.

On August 1st 2002 Tony and I went to Pride Park to play a mascots match in front of the Queen as part of her Golden Jubilee celebrations hosted by

Buxton man Tim Brooke Taylor there was a full day of celebrations with the doors opening at midday and throughout the afternoon there were 2000 Derbyshire children in a unique cavalcade, the Derbyshire City and County Youth Band and an 180 strong choir the Red Devils also made an appearance, Dave Mackay was there with the 1974/5 Championship winning side, Ellen McArthur the Derbyshire born yachtswoman and fifty Four renowned local gymnasts, 280 dancers, 1000lb of fireworks, 1000000 pieces of confetti and forty two cuddly mascots taking part in a twenty one a side soccer match there were also many stalls and events taking place outside the stadium. The Queen arrived at 2:45 pm, the match kicked off at 3pm and it poured with rain all afternoon, a typical August day, but that did not stop over 27000 people watching in the stadium. The costumes got heavier and heavier as they got wetter and wetter and mascots were slipping and sliding everywhere it was hilarious and as the Charlton mascots were there again trying to avoid each other and playing the match was virtually impossible. Sadly we did not get to meet the Queen afterwards but who can blame her.

On a wet and cold Saturday November 11th 2002, we travelled to Ashton Gate for a League 2 match against Bristol City. Conditions were awful and Mrs Magpie (on my own again sadly) got soaked before kick off and at half time as I slipped and slid everywhere trying to avoid the standing water. Paul Heffernan had put Notts in front when in the 49th minute the referee abandoned the match. The one and only time in all my years watching Notts away from home that a game I was at was abandoned. The game was rearranged for Tuesday December 3rd but by then we were on a family holiday in Australia. It was very weird laying on Bondi beach in the sunshine as text alerts came through for the rearranged match which Notts went on to lose 3:2 Mark Stallard putting Notts in front on 19 minutes and equalising on 80 minutes at 2:2 only for Bristol City to get an 83rd minute winner. On December 15th whilst in Sydney we went to a day night one day international between Australia and England. Australia won the toss elected to bat and never looked back amassing 318/6 in their 50 overs. England were never in it and finished on 229 all out! But it was a great experience especially as the sun set and the beer flowed and it was so cheap! No more than £10! I asked why and the answer I got was "the population of Australia is so small that if we raised the prices we wouldn't fill the grounds" logical thinking I suppose?

Saturday February 8th 2003 saw me undertake one of my tougher challenges as a mascot and this one totally self inflicted Mr and Mrs Magpie and the Junior Magpies decided to walk the 17 plus miles from Meadow Lane to Field Mill for the match. A crazy idea from the start but why not? We set off from Meadow Lane about 8am we being Mr Magpie Tony, Mrs Magpie me, my son Daniel, my Daughter Kimberley, Iris Smith, Alan Higgott, Gary Seagrave and his children Luke and Oliver, Keith from Worcester and Neil Mason. Loraine was running the support car (if I have missed anybody I apologise). Off we went round Meadow Lane up London Road then Glasshouse Street and onto Mansfield Road. My bus driving colleagues loved it and kept honking and waving. Through Sherwood we went then through Arnold up to Redhill until we got to the Leapools Roundabout where the road divides (straight on for the A614 to Doncaster and left for the A60 to Mansfield) and I committed my cardinal sin. We were doing so well we stopped for refreshments at the Little Chef by the roundabout. All the sensible people had water I thought I would be clever and have a hot chocolate despite the fact I had not eaten all day. Not a great idea! after about half an hour on we went past the Half way house and on to Newstead Abbey gates where my hot chocolate decided to make a re appearance so I had to drop out having managed nearly twelve of the seventeen miles. Wimp! Everybody else made it to Field Mill and credit to them all, but maybe I am glad I didn't feel to clever, Notts lost 3:2 Mark Stallard scoring two late goals to make the score look respectable having been three down. The next home game was on Saturday the 15th February 2003 when we beat Bristol City 2:0 with goals from Mark Stallard and Paul Heffernan. We were all on the pitch at half time and I put my hand in my pocket and bought all those who had completed the walk a trophy and again congratulated them all.

In May 2003 Loraine got her dream job working at Meadow Lane in the Conference and Banqueting Suites. Preparing rooms for conferences, as well as serving meals to the players were just some of her duties and she had many happy years there. On Sunday 27th July 2003 Mr and Mrs Magpie were invited to Rockingham motor racing circuit in Northamptonshire to take part in a mascot race during their ASCAR Stock Car racing meeting. This was run on a banked oval with 32000 people in attendance. Not only were the mascots invited but the Supporters Club were given 50 complimentary tickets as well so a good few of us turned up on the day. Neither Tony nor Sheena was available to wear the costume that day so once we arrived and were shown to an executive box with a fabulous view of the finishing straight, it was decided Daniel would do it and as I as usual had no chance of winning I willingly gave up my costume to his friend Ashley Storey. We must have missed something on the invitation as it was not a foot race but you could use any form of non-motorised transport. Rocky the Rhino the Rockingham mascot and Poacher from Lincoln City had Bicycles (needless to say they came first and second). Cyril the Swan tried a skateboard Elvis J Eel and Sammy the Shrimp used an Industrial size Wheelie Bin, Elvis inside and Sammy pushing. Deepdale Duck from Preston had a motorised skate board that he couldn't start. Also competing were another dozen football mascots and the London Knight from the London Knights Ice Hockey Team (he finished third). We watched this race and the high speed racing from the box but were also allowed to wander round the pits where all the teams and owners were and where if we wanted we could have any pieces of the fibre glass that had come off the cars and if we were lucky the drivers would sign them for us. It appeared that football mascots had taken off in a big way and Mr & Mrs Magpie to a lesser extent couldn't get enough of the fun.

Just over three years after the first 24 hour football marathon, I was arranging another Junior Magpies 24 hour Football Marathon, this time at Sport Nottingham on the indoor pitch above the Meadow Club with the squash courts being used to sleep in. This time we were raising money for the club and more especially we had been asked to buy towels for the players, amongst other things. This time the teams were split into "far end" and "near end". It was set to start at 6pm on Saturday 25th October 2003 after the home game against Brentford, which Notts won 2:0 thanks to Clive Platt and Darren Caskey. This put everyone in high spirits to start with and it was also the FA Cup first round draw (we got a Home tie against Shildon). More reason for high spirits. By 6pm there were 14 Junior Magpies (aged 6-12) and 25 Senior Juniors (aged 12-18) taking part and throughout the marathon there were 13 people over 20 playing. Billy Dearden and his grandson Matthew came to start the first game, adding to the fun happy atmosphere and we were off but it was around this moment it was pointed out to me and everybody taking part that on October 25th 2003 British Summertime was ending and the clocks were going to be put back 1 hour so even before we got into our marathon it was now going to last for 25 hours. Doom and gloom set in and everybody blamed me, as usual, oh well it was warm and dry so we would just have to get on with it. Again the games were planned in 20 minute intervals, with Alan Higgott the referee for all the time he wasn't playing and me doing the scoring. This time the first goal was scored by Marcus Eaton (yes him again). By 8pm Loraine had been to McDonald's on Radcliffe Road as they had kindly donated Burgers and Fries again. The food was gratefully received as the ball kept rolling and as we were indoors we had no problems keeping the marathon going despite the extra hour we had to play although there was very little sleep throughout the night. Again bacon and sausage sandwiches appeared about 8am on Sunday morning and again they were gratefully received. Because of the extra hour and because we were indoors and the weather was not a problem, we scored an extra 201 goals than last time. Daniel Walster score the 1152nd goal tying the previous effort at 3:27 on Sunday afternoon and within a couple of minutes Luke Brassfield had set a new high score. The extra hour ultimately did not make that much difference just the novelty value of playing a 25 hour 24 hour soccer marathon. As we approached the last few minutes Nick Fenton and Kevin Nicholson came to join us to encourage us and at the final whistle they presented the certificates and trophies. The final goal was scored by Tom Openshaw and by the end the score was "Far End" 695:650 "Near End" not a draw this time even though last time was not a manufactured score. Just quite strange.

This time the scorers were:

FAR END:		NEAR END:	
Daniel Belcher	55 +1 OG	Jamie Foster	58
Jamie Foster	54	Jamie Monk	57
Ashley Storey	54 + 1 OG	Mark Hosker	49

Matthew Taylor	51	Colin Lanes	44
Carl Bates	48	Carl Bates	40
Marcus Eaton	43	Daniel Belcher	39
Martin Walters	37	Ryan Andrew	39
Dan Walster	31 +1 OG	Luke Brassfield	31
Colin Lanes	28	Dan Walster	29
Jamie Monk	28	Marcus Eaton	27
Stefan Fisher	28 + 1 OG	Martin Walters	27
Liam Platt	22	Adam Hosker	25
Ryan Humphrey	19	David Wilson	19
Ryan Andrews	16	Ryan Humphrey	18
Jake Pitt	16	Luke Webster	13
Luke Webster	15	Charlotte Taylor	12
Andrew Bowler	12	Ashley Storey	11
Luke Brassfield	11	Dan Goldsmith	8
Mark Hosker	10 +1 OG	Matthew Taylor	8
Adam Dallison	10	Liam Platt	8
David Wilson	9	Alan Higgott	8 +1 OG
Norm Worthington	9 +1 OG	Martin Hall	6
AlanHiggott	7 +2 OG	Nathan Crossman	6
Martin Hall	7	Luke Seagrave	6
Dan Goldsmith	6 +1 OG	Martin Quinn	6
Kev Humphrey	6 +1 OG	Stefan Fisher	5
Gary Seagrave	6 +1 OG	Gary Seagrave	5
Luke Seagrave	6	Jake Pitt	4
Tom Openshaw	5	Gemma Hemsley	4
Tony Walster	5	Loraine Walster	4
Malc Shearstone	5	Jermaine Worthington	3
Adam Hosker	5	Adam Dallison	3
Jermaine Worthington	4	Tony Walster	3
Nigel Webster	3	Keenan Belcher	2
Keenan Belcher	3	Ian Openshaw	2
Martin Quinn	3	Kev Humphrey	2

Kim Walster	2	Andrew Bowler	2
Lisa Doleman	2	Tom Openshaw	1
Nathan Crossman	2	Aaron Belcher	1
Gemma Hemsley	2	Robin Wheatley Smith	1
Charlotte Taylor	2	Charlie Wheatley Smith	1
Stuart Wright	2		
Taylor Belcher	1		
Matthew Wheat	1		
Melissa Humphrey	1 +2 OG		
Ian Openshaw	1		
Charlie Wheatley Smith	1		

FAR END 694 + 1 OG = 695   NEAR END 637 + 13 OG = 650

The Far End were good enough to score 13 goals for the Near End they reciprocated with just the one but this time there was a result. This time the leading scorer was Jamie Foster a twelve year old Forest fan with 112 goals. Thank you to him and everybody else who took part in the 25 hour 24 hour football marathon, especially those who had now done this twice. We raised enough money for the club to get the towels they wanted. Notts County had been in administration since June 2002 and by September 2003 were given a final three months stay of execution by the FA after studying details of a takeover however monies still had to be raised by any means possible and all Notts fans did their bit.

On Sunday October 5th 2003 Notts County Legends faced Nottingham Forest Legends at Meadow Lane in an effort to raise funds. The crowd was 8,702 with the kick off having to be delayed 15 minutes to allow the people in. Mr and Mrs Magpie were in attendance buckets in hand as was Sherwood Bear. As we were on the pitch before the game, I had an idea and having got permission from the club and from Sherwood himself put it into operation. As the match got underway along with Tony we "locked" Sherwood up in one of the cells under the Family Stand borrowed his head and went round the pitch side telling all the supporters we had kidnapped

Sherwood and they would have to pay to get him released. It worked a treat as supporters of both clubs put money in our buckets some even throwing money into Sherwood's head and by the time we went off to get Sherwood back and prepare for half time our buckets were each more than half full. Thank you to everybody who contributed. Sherwood was duly "released" and back on the pitch with us. The match finished Notts County Legends 3 Nottingham Forest Legends 2, Garry Birtles with an early goal before a Tommy Johnson goal made it 1:1 at half time. Kevin Bartlett and then a Phil Stant penalty put Notts in control before a late goal from Ian McParland set up a thrilling finish Notts County legends eventually winning 3:2. More importantly over £40000 was raised. Notts considering their perilous financial situation and shocking league form were handed a major financial lifeline on Wednesday October 29th 2003 when they travelled to Stamford Bridge to play Chelsea in the League Cup third round. I asked Iris to see if the mascots could attend and surprise surprise the answer was no as it was at most top flight clubs, this would explain why very few of their mascots were ever seen at mascot events throughout the country. So along with many thousands of other supporters I boarded a coach at Meadow Lane and headed South in hope not in expectation and in all honesty the hope was of not getting humiliated more than anything else. Once we arrived a group of us started singing "we are only here for the money" and "we came all this way because we are skint" which got picked up by BBC East Midlands Today. I am delighted to say we appeared on television on the Thursday evening. Everyone knows the score 4:2 to Chelsea with Notts in the game until the last few minutes when Chelsea scored their fourth in a real thriller. Suffice to say my whole game was ruined by the woman in the seat next to me who although dressed in black and white from head to toe had obviously never been to a Notts game I would suggest before in her life so spent the whole game asking the man next to her "Who is that? What was that for? What happened there?" I know we needed all the support we could get but it was so off putting I couldn't enjoy the game at all. Just my luck.

On November 22nd 2003 Mr and Mrs Magpie along with Sherwood the Bear were invited to take part in the Christmas light switch on at the Council house. Billy Dearden and Paul Hart the respective managers were going to be there and Darren Caskey and Nick Fenton along with Andy Reid and

Marlon Harewood also made an appearance. The mascots changed in the Theatre Royal changing rooms and then along with all the dignitaries such as the Lord Mayor we caught the tram being driven by "Santa Claus" the one stop down Market Street to the square heading for the Council House. The tram was not in service at this time, and wouldn't be for another six months at least but this is still the only time I have ever used it, before disembarking and walking through the large crowds of people to the Council House. Once inside the Council House the estimated 7000+ crowd were entertained by the Nottingham Youth Theatre Singers, a local band called Traphic and Radio Trent Breakfast Show DJs JO and TWIGGY. Twiggy being dressed as an elf. At this time Jo and Twiggy were on the pitch at half time during every game at Meadow Lane. We all made our way upstairs to the Ballroom where food and drink had been provided and where I linked up with Loraine and the children again. The time came for the switch on and everyone was ushered to the balcony in order of importance which sadly meant there was little room for the mascots but Tony and I did our best to make ourselves seen. I honestly have no idea if we were or not but the banquet and drinks afterwards made up for it. During the next couple of weeks I was present at the light switch on in Arnold, Netherfield and Carlton. The mascot phenomena was growing throughout the country but how long would it last? I didn't know or care at the time, I was just happy and proud to represent Notts County all around the country.

On Saturday March 13th 2004 and a Supporters Club trip to Adams Park Wycombe, not as mascot this time but just to watch the game. When I left HMS Newcastle one of my colleagues a Radio Operator got me a Union Flag as I had asked him and left it in a locker at Plymouth Railway Station. I was expecting a fairly small flag so imagine my surprise when I got to the locker and found a huge flag, double quilt size at least nine foot by six foot. I took it anyway and having put the club name through the middle of it (I have to confess it was many years later that it was pointed out to me the flag was upside down) we took it with us to away games including this one. I put it over the rail at the edge of the pitch and within minutes a steward asked me politely enough if I could move it as it was blocking the advertising hoardings that people had paid for. I moved it and asked if I could lay it on the grass behind the pitch? Whether he heard me or not I have no idea as he was already walking away but I did just that. Ten minutes or so later a Senior Steward walked up to me and his opening line was "is this yours?", pointing to the flag and having confirmed that it was, the next thing he said took me completely by surprise "Is it fireproofed?", he asked. I had to ask him again just to make sure I had heard properly but sure enough that's what he asked. I said "I honestly have no idea but it is MOD issue so I would have thought so wouldn't you?" To which his reply was "have you got a certificate to prove it?" Again I told him it was MOD issue so where do I get a certificate?" His reply was "You need to take it to a dry cleaners any dry cleaners they will fireproof it for you and then give you a certificate." My reply was "It's just approaching 2:40, I honestly don't think I would have time before kick-off but I will make sure to get it done next week" This was not good enough as his response was "move it now" to which my response was "those three flags in the home end have they all got certificates?" On confirmation of this I said "could I see one please so I know what they look like"? His reply was "no you can't! Who do you think you are?" Now out you go you and your flag" and with that he manhandled me towards the exit gates while his mate bought my flag. By now I was more than a little unimpressed but kept my cool and once out the ground I put the flag on the coach and went back to the gate where the kindly gate man let me back in. On asking if the steward was always that pleasant to visiting supporters he confirmed "yes always". Notts got a draw taking the lead with a Paul Heffernan goal before being pegged back and to my eternal delight, Wycombe finished bottom of the league at the end of that season and sadly, NOT, were relegated. Notts finished second bottom and were also relegated but that is a ground I have no intention of ever returning to. After the final game of the season in May 2004 a 1:1 draw at home to Oldham with a last minute equaliser by Defender Tony Barras, the costumes were sent again for their end of season clean. Not to the same dry cleaners this time and with the understanding that they were needed again by early July for the Sport Relief Mile at Wollaton Park. Good to their word the costumes were collected on Monday July 5th 2004 with no dramas at all.

This turned out to be quite convenient because on Friday 9th I received a phone call from Natalie Jackson at BBC East Midlands Today asking if Mr and Mrs Magpie could make it to Wollaton Park for about 5:30pm to be filmed "sparring" with Carl Froch to promote the fact that the following afternoon it was planned for Mrs Magpie to go in the ring with him for a "fun" bout. He is a local boxer, who had won and retained the Commonwealth Super Middleweight title earlier in the year, winning it on March 12th 2004 by beating Charles Adamu on points and taking his professional record to 12 and 0. He retained it on June 2nd 2004 by beating Mark Woolnaugh by TKO and maintaining his unbeaten record now 13 and 0. Froch along with Martin Johnson the England and Leicester Tigers Rugby Union Captain were the celebrities taking part in Nottingham. Sadly Mr Magpie was unavailable on the Friday but I arrived with plenty of time and changed long before I was needed. I was introduced to Mr Froch by Natalie, I must admit at the time I had never heard of him and apparently he was a Forest supporter! That is debatable as in his later autobiography he states he does not like football but chose to be a Forest fan as they have a larger fan base and hopefully that would encourage more people to come and watch him fight. As 6:30pm chimed we were filmed shaking hand and wing, that was easy but as the sport news started and the cameras were running we were supposed to start sparring and things got a bit more difficult. I was Mrs Magpie the Notts County mascot, he was a professional boxer and a Forest fan and he did not hold back to much wearing gloves that evening. The costume may have been padded but not that well, I ached for many days afterwards and was supposed to get in the ring with him the next day. The things we do for charity! Saturday afternoon I arrived back at Wollaton Park with Loraine and my children Daniel 16 and Kimberley 14, I found somewhere to change and as Mr Magpie was still unavailable Kimberley had volunteered to wear the costume to help out. In mid-afternoon I set off with the family to "run the mile" There were many people taking part (throughout the afternoon 4100 people took part) and I am pleased to say that for the first part of the mile, the uphill part towards the hall, Mr and Mrs Magpie were the centre of attention making running all but impossible, pictures wanting to be taken and questions having to be answered and just general conversation being the priority but as we reached the top of the hill and turned around to do the last part of the run downhill I decided to "go for it" and ran as fast as I could not that fast but it did feel that I overtook many people probably a dozen at most and I was delighted to realise I had beaten both Loraine and Kimberley to the finish line. (Poor Kimberley didn't stand a chance, the costume was much bigger than her and she was not used to wearing it and it was also very hot.) No idea if I beat Daniel in all honesty but even so with the run finished and with a bit of trepidation, I made my way to the boxing ring that had been set up and met Martin Johnson for the first time. All I can say is wow he had the biggest hands I had and have ever seen in my life. I must admit for the only time in the years I was Mrs Magpie, I did not want to be there, but it was for charity. Hope Mr Froch remembered that! But then something miraculous happened, for a reason I never did find out the boxing was cancelled, I was that delighted I could have run the mile again but thought better of it. I rushed off to get Kimberley and we both changed before anyone changed their mind and spent the rest of the afternoon enjoying the fun along with all those present.

Organised by Val Nicholson, mum of Professional footballer Shane Nicholson. Collingham FC hosted an annual charity match it was first started in 1998 raising funds for Newark's Beaumond House Community Hospice where her husband Ian Nicholson had passed away in 1996. Mr Nicholson was a former player and still involved in the running of the club up until his death. Cast and crew from the television soap Emmerdale provided the opposition every year, giving their time for free, and on Sunday 5th September 2004 the mascots were invited to entertain and take part in an "It's a Knockout" contest before the charity match kicked off. The usual suspects turned up Lenny City Gent Bradford City, Captain Blade Sheffield United, Poacher The Imp Lincoln City, Benny the Buck Telford United, Yorkie the Lion York City, Moonchester Manchester City, Lenny Lion Shrewsbury Town, Billy Brewer Boston United Whaddney Cheltenham Town and of course Mrs Magpie. Sadly I could not get anybody to come as Mr Magpie yet again. We changed in a small room next to the club house and off we went into the sunshine to see what we had to do. We had to negotiate obstacle courses, sprint across the pitch and throw a shot amongst other things. Needless to say as usual Mrs Magpie came nearer last than first but it was tremendous fun despite the fact it was a boiling hot day. Once the fun had finished we all went back to change and watch the charity football match. Even Paul Gascoigne, who was manager of Boston United at the time, turned up to spectate and donate a signed shirt to Collingham FC. Once the game had finished we all headed back into the club house for a drink and some food, kindly laid on by the club. Then disaster struck Benny the Buck went to retrieve his costume as he had to go home and he couldn't find his head. Not a rare occurrence when we change in such confined spaces so we all went back with him to look in our own kit bags and around. Sure enough his head was nowhere to be found. Why on earth would anybody want to steal a mascots head? We couldn't understand but Benny, who did a lot of charity work so needed the head was very upset and insisted on calling the police who arrived a short while later to take statements from all of us. The head never did reappear and Benny resorted to making a temporary head out of a cardboard box with two bananas as antlers. When we all met up again at the Mascot Grand National at Huntingdon, Benny had got head. A lady from the USA had heard about the theft and had sent the money to get it replaced.

Notts always seem to get local matches the week before Christmas and so it was on Saturday December 18th 2004 we found ourselves at the Vetch Field playing Swansea City. Mrs Magpie was there on her own again sadly and Kim, my daughter was my assistant, helping me get ready but sadly not carrying the costumes. As usual and understandably we changed in a store room at the home end and then Cyril the Swan and I did our bit on the pitch before kick-off. Once the match had started we changed again and Cyril took me upstairs to a bar to watch the first half on television completely forgetting about Kim, who at 14 was amongst the home fans in her Notts shirt. It wasn't until she came to find me about 25 minutes into the game that I remembered and by then Cyril and I had consumed a drink or two. Kim stayed with me until half time then we changed again and went back out on the pitch, did our bit, then changed back again. At the time Cyril was sponsored by "Monster Munch" and the room we were changing in was full of boxes of Monster Munches. Cyril said "help yourself to as many as you want, we can't get rid of the damned things" I filled the quilt cover with as many boxes as I could especially the "Flaming Hot" ones, as they were my favourites and made my way round the pitch in shorts and T shirt with a very full double quilt over my shoulder. Tim Lovejoy of SOCCER AM fame showed a clip of it the next week on the show and wanted to know who I was and what I was carrying. That was the highlight of the day as Swansea ran out 4:0 winners, a certain Lee Trundle scoring a hat trick.

Easter weekend 2005 saw Notts at home to Bristol Rovers on Saturday 26th March 2005 suffering a 2:1 defeat with Glynn Hurst giving us an early lead before Rovers turned it all around. After the game the family travelled down to my parents in Worcester to spend Easter with them and on Easter Monday I took the family to St Georges Lane to watch Worcester City record a fine 3:0 victory over Hucknall Town. On Tuesday 29th we drove to Yeovil to watch Notts who were in 20th place in the league take on the league leaders on their own pitch. It was a shocking day, pouring with rain, and the away end at Yeovil was open to the elements, but as the game progressed this mattered less and less. Stefan Oakes put Notts in front early in the game with an absolute screamer of a goal before Glynn Hurst scored to put us 2:0 ahead at half time. Mark Stallard added a third before Yeovil scored a late penalty, Notts running out 3:1 winners. Soaked to the skin I didn't care and celebrated at the end as if we had just been promoted.

On Sunday May 22nd 2005 along with the family I drove to Loftus Road for an event called The Big Kick-about A Scout Day Out, hosted by ex-Blue Peter presenter Peter Duncan who was promoted to Chief Scout on 4th September 2004. It was a chance for the public to meet the stars and join in the fun. There were footballing tips from QPR players past and present, mascot fun and games and kick-about goodies. Everyone present was given a Friendship Band and a sew on badge like a scout badge to commemorate the day (sadly I have absolutely no idea where either of those is) It was hectic and very very sunny so wearing the costume was a nightmare.

Saturday 6th August 2005 saw the start of a new season and a trip to Torquay. We would make a full day of it having already rung to find out and have it confirmed that Mr and Mrs Magpie would be able to attend. We set off early in convoy my four and Karl Simms (affectionately known as Stumpy) in our car with Gary Seagrave, Neil Mason and Gary's children, Luke and Oliver in his. We arrived at Babbacombe by 10am parking up and meeting up with our friends from Worcester and fellow Notts fans Keith and Carol. Yes Notts fans from Worcester, if only I had known them thirty years ago but that's your luck. Karl has Multiple Sclerosis and usually uses crutches but on bad days he lets me push him in his wheelchair, the fool! Carol has very bad Osteo-Artheritis and again can walk but usually uses a mobility scooter. So it was in Babbacombe and having been to a cafe for breakfast we decided to try and find the beach. We found a narrow path going downwards very steeply but thought with the wheelchair and scooter we could get down to the sand. Sadly that didn't happen as the brakes on Carol's scooter failed and she hurtled down the path out of control. She had the sense to steer left into the fence, who knows what would have happened if she had carried on, and brought her scooter to a halt by crashing into the fence. We all thought the worst but thankfully she wasn't badly injured. Even so Keith took her to the local hospital and the rest of us went back up the hill and headed to the club at the ground for a drink. Amazingly Keith and Carol were back with us before I headed off to do my mascot duties, I found my way to the reception and was told that Torquay didn't welcome away mascots I tried to explain it was already arranged but the lady was adamant I couldn't do it. Oh well not the first time! On the way out of the reception I bumped into Eamonn Holmes the television star, he was performing at Torquay at the time and was going on the pitch at half time. He is a lot smaller than you would think and with the greatest respect a bit chubbier than he looks on television.

The following day Sunday 7th August 2005 we found ourselves back at Rockingham Motor Racing Circuit in Northamptonshire at another Motor Racing event this time SCSA (Stock Car Speed Association) but things had changed (it had been boycotted by the mascots the year before because with no tickets being offered, even for the mascot, the majority felt they were being used) This year there was only a ticket for the mascot and helper and very few "genuine" mascots turned up. There was a mascot dressed in track suit and running shoes and a balaclava supposedly a monkey representing Finedon Volta, who were they? But he had won the Mascot Grand National the year before and was local. The fun was rapidly being taken out of things it was now win at all cost. Seven actual mascots turned up. Mr and Mrs Magpie, Poacher and Mrs Poacher from Lincoln, Benny Buck from Telford, Billy Brewer from Burton and Bodger from Wycombe Wanderers, as well as Rocky the Rhino the Rockingham mascot and the Finedon Volta monkey. Finedon Volta being a team in the 11th or 12 tier of the football pyramid so of course they needed a mascot. This time it was an obstacle course along the finishing straight with Gary Seagrave and Daniel competing in the Magpie costumes and they came first and second. They actually got to stand on the top two steps of the podium to receive their trophies and medals from the Hooters girls! It was fantastic and the champagne went down rather well to.

Saturday September 17th 2005 saw us at Gay Meadow to watch Notts minus mascot costumes as it was my birthday game. The season had started well Notts being unbeaten in their first eight league games, winning four and drawing four, so hopes were high despite the fact this was my annual birthday match. Although it wasn't on my actual birthday these games have never been lucky. Gay Meadow it turns out was my most visited away ground at the time although I have not been to their new ground yet. I drove on the understanding Loraine would drive home so I could have a beer or two and as Daniel had turned eighteen a week earlier there was a possibility even he would buy me a drink. It didn't happen and very rarely if ever has since. We also took Karl with us and were parked up in the car park behind the away end by midday. Getting Karl in his chair and with me pushing we walked the short distance to the Crown Inn to enjoy some lunchtime hospitality. A few drinks were enjoyed and about 2:45 we decided it was time to watch the match so with Karl, again in his chair and me pushing, that is where we headed. Once at the away end Karl decided he didn't want to go in the ground in his chair but would use his crutches so I put the chair back in the car and bought his crutches for him. As we were let through the gates the teams were coming out so Karl decided to be clever and not use the steps at the edge of the terracing but to climb up the bank at the front. Needless to say he went tumbling, much to every ones amusement including his own. Once I had picked him up he tried again with the same results and even more laughter. Eventually we were in our place and watching the game just as Notts missed three glorious chances before being punished not once but twice by Shrewsbury and going in at half time 2:0 down. In the second half Notts were awarded a penalty which was taken by Julian Baudet. In goal for Shrewsbury was a youngster called Joe Hart who pulled off a great save right in front of us. Baudet took ten penalties in his career, eight for Notts, and he missed three in total, two for Notts. That wasn't the end of it either in the last minute Baudet and Kelvin Langmead of Shrewsbury were sent off and the birthday curse continued, Notts lost their unbeaten start to the season.

Sunday 26th September 2005 saw Mr and Mrs Magpies last visit to the Mascot Grand National. Things were changing and not for the better. The Sun newspaper had always been part of the day with page 3 girls in attendance but this year they entered a racer wearing a fancy dress mask and running shoes. The runner inside the Chaddy the Owl costume (Oldham Athletic) was an extra from Coronation Street, who came to blows with Captain Blade (Sheffield United) half way down the course. Suddenly it was win at all costs and no more free reign to entertain the crowd. The feeling amongst the genuine football mascots was they were being exploited as between 2004 and 2010 not one genuine football mascot won the race. The football mascots had made the race what it was. When it started in 1999 there were 17 football mascots taking part. By 2005 there were well over 100 but at least half of them had no connection with a football club. The bubble had burst. By 2009 the racecourse were happy to run it with very few if any football mascots at all.

Saturday November 18th 2005 was Children in Need Day and the East Midlands programme was being broadcast live from the Departures Lounge at East Midlands Airport coinciding with the 40th anniversary of the Airport being opened. It was presented from 6pm by Anne Davies and Richard Arnold. The evening was jungle themed and the Departure Lounge was filled with wooden huts and large plants. Also in attendance were an African Dance Troupe called The Mighty Zulu Nation and an Asian Band of Drummers. There was also a Gospel Choir, the Derbyshire Teenage Group Forgotten, Loughborough Universities Tuxedo Swing Orchestra and a satellite link to Southwell Minster, where the choir sang Tears In Heaven written by Eric Clapton and originally released in 1992. Also present were most of the Regional Mascots from Rammie (Derby County), Filbert Fox (Leicester City), Sherwood (Forest), Mr and Mrs Magpie and of course Pudsey Bear to name but a few. This time instead of the Greyhound Track we had to run across the car park and this time my form returned and I came nearer the back than the front but made sure I beat Sherwood. Sheena who was in Mr Magpies costume did little better but the crowd had a great laugh which is the whole idea. Back inside the Departures Lounge we continued interacting with the public but at some stage of the evening I managed to get a dance with Anne Davies.

On Friday January 13th 2006 (yes Friday 13th) disaster struck in my personal life! I was sitting at home with Loraine on a Friday evening watching A Question of Sport and I turned to her because I knew an answer. I could hear myself talking but all I saw was Loraine grab for the phone. My face had dropped on one side and my speech was slurred. Loraine thought I was having a Stroke and rang for an ambulance. I felt fine. By 8pm the ambulance was outside I was taken inside where they examined me for a good hour before going back in the house and suggesting to Loraine that as it was Friday evening and A and E may well be busy they didn't think I needed to go to hospital. I never went and by 9:30pm we were in our local club, A place we visited every Friday as I was the bingo caller my wages being two pints. It transpired when I visited my GP on the Monday I had had a TIA (Transient Ischaemic Attack) or mild stroke so I was lucky, but it cost me my PSV Licence and with 12 weeks' notice I lost my job driving buses at NCT. Irony of irony on the day I left Friday 7th April 2006 I was presented with my NVQ Level 2 certificate. I had completed my NVQ Level 2 in Road Passenger Transport on December 21st 2005 and the presentation day was April 7th. So no job, bad health, but an NVQ Level 2 certificate. Not all bad then! It was suggested by NCT Marketing Director Nicola Tidy that if I was interested Nottinghamshire County Cricket Club were looking for somebody to be their new mascot, NUTS the squirrel. I jumped at the chance although my priority was obviously to try and find a job as soon as possible. The squirrel costume was amazingly far heavier than the Magpies costume and the tail could possibly have been described as a "dangerous weapon" it was so big and cumbersome. I did a photo shoot in costume with Graeme Swann and Stephen Flemimg in an open topped Lexus at Lady Bay and a couple of days later, on Friday June 2nd 2006 on the first day of the Third Test between England and Sri Lanka. NUTS was introduced to the Nation in a Live Press Conference on SKY Sports from Trent Bridge, sitting between Captain Stephen Fleming and Graeme Swann. It was all tremendous fun but if I am honest my heart was not totally in the job. I appeared in costume at all four T20 group matches against Durham, Yorkshire, Derbyshire and Leicestershire, all of which Notts won on their way to the final. But by the quarter finals I had relinquished my post!

Just after leaving my job, Notts had one of the most important games in their history, the last game of the 2005/6 season on 6th May2006 at home to

Bury, with more than a chance of getting relegated out of the football league. Unthinkable was the biased "black and white" thinking but the reality was it could and very nearly did happen. Kevin Humphrey and I did mascot that day but our hearts were not in it at all. Everyone was to nervous. I had taken the family to Hereford on May 3rd 1997 when they played Brighton on the last game of the season with the loser dropping out the league. It finished 1:1 and Hereford were relegated on goals scored. Notts had already been relegated so we went to Edgar Street instead of Chesterfield. That was disappointing enough as a half-hearted Hereford supporter but I knew how bad the feeling was and no way did I want that to happen again. By half time nerves were beyond shredded. Bury were winning 1:0 with a goal on 41 minutes. I went to get changed and cried my eyes out over Notts County for the second time in my life. Worse was to come on the 81st minute Bury went 2 up. Was it all over for the club? But no, on 86 minutes Dan Martin got one back and then in the 89th minute Notts were awarded a penalty. Julian Baudet stepped up and we were safe. It finished 2:2, as it happened results elsewhere went our way and even if we had lost we would have been safe although not many people knew that until later. The majority in the 9817 crowd celebrated like we had won the cup after the final whistle. What a great finish to an awful day.

Sharon Beshenivsky was a West Yorkshire Police Constable, PC 6410 shot dead by a gang during a robbery in Bradford on Friday 18th November 2005. She was 38 years old and had only served 9 months as a police officer at the time of her death. WPC Beshenivsky along with her colleague WPC Teresa Millburn responded to reports that an attack alarm had been activated at a Travel Agents in Bradford. Upon arrival the two WPCs encountered three men who had robbed the agent of £5,405.00, two were armed with a gun and one with a knife. One of the gunmen fired at point blank range fatally wounding Beshenivsky in the chest and wounding Millburn before they made their getaway. Sharon Beshenivsky became the 7th WPC to die in the Line of Duty and the first to die in an "ordinary" gun crime. She died on her youngest daughter's 4th birthday. On Monday May 1st 2006 Mr and Mrs Magpie took part in a Mascot V Mascot football match, in aid of Sharon Beshenivsky's family, at Valley Parade the home of Bradford City FC. I travelled up with the family but nobody to do Mr Magpie. In the end

Kimberley not for the first time stepped into the breach I was so proud of her as it was a very hot day but it was for a tremendous cause. Lenny the City Gent the Bradford mascot, not only has one of the best mascot costumes there is, (the Bradford City Strip a bowler hat and an umbrella so no problem with visibility or breathing there) but he is also one of the nicest mascots I have ever come across, a True Gent. The match was starting at 2pm and in the next hours 25 to 35 mascots turned up from as far afield as Blackpool Bloomfield Bear to Plymouth Pilgrim Pete as well as many other regulars such as Deepdale Duck from Preston, Yorkie from York City, Moonchester from Manchester City, Captain Blade from Sheffield United, Chaddy the Owl from Oldham, Lenny the Lion from Shrewsbury, Billy the Brewer from Burton Albion Whaddney from Cheltenham and Benny the Buck from AFC Telford. A dafter funnier group of people I have yet to meet. We changed in one of the function rooms, the only place large enough to accommodate all of us, and by 1:30 we were all out on the pitch playing to the crowd and what a crowd, there must have been over 10,000 people there. The match was played in brilliant sunshine, all we needed, and at times it was 15 a side and at times at least 18 a side and at times 5 a side as the weather took its toll but the important thing was to entertain the crowd as best we could. As always happened Mr and Mrs Magpie were on the same side and not Lenny's side so although our side won we lost, as the host mascot could NEVER lose.

On a very sunny Tuesday August 22nd 2006, with a full car consisting of myself Loraine Dan Kim and Karl Simms (Stumpy) we met Gary Seagrave and Neil Mason and Gary's children Luke and Oliver outside Meadow Lane at about 3pm to drive in convoy down to Crystal Palace FC in South London for Round One of the League Cup. I led and we got into the middle of London about 5pm it was a fabulously sunny day and we had all windows open and Meatloaf Bat Out of Hell playing on the CD Player as we drove past the Oval Surrey's cricket ground. I was in what I thought was the outside lane but turned out to be the oncoming traffic lane! There was a large white van heading towards me and the left hand lane was full of traffic, what could I do? Not a clue! The screams from the back of the car just galvanised me more and shutting my eyes I took my chances. I have no real idea what happened suffice to say we survived. So unscathed we parked at

Selhurst park I took Karl in his wheelchair and we watched a fabulous game, Notts going one down but winning 2:1 with goals by Lawrie Dudfield and Dan Martin. Even the steward was cheering Notts on as he did not fancy extra time and possibly penalties. After a fabulous result we went back to the car and Loraine asked if on the way home we could go past Harrods? Why not? so as she was navigating that is what we did and having seen the lights, we drove on. Ten minutes later we were driving past Harrods again and ten minutes later we passed it a third time. That was enough for me so I took on the navigating and driving. As we approached Staples Corner, Karl decided he was hungry so finding a fish and chip shop I pulled over. Loraine went for the food, Karl wanted sausage chips and gravy. He got his sausage and chips but sadly when gravy was asked for all we got was blank looks. Phillistines!

On Friday October 20th 2006 Mr and Mrs Magpie did what was to prove to be their last birthday party. A 40th for good friend and fellow Notts fan, Gary Ratcliffe at Turners above the Co-op on Mapperley top. I had to find somebody to wear the other costume so step forward Gary Seagrave again. We changed in the stair well leading up to Turners (I had changed in far worse places) hoping that nobody would be coming up or down (luckily they didn't) and then made our way upstairs. The look on Gary's face was priceless and made it all worthwhile. My one big regret as mascot is that I didn't do more birthday parties only the three in 10 years and only the one sanctioned by the Supporters Club, a 21st birthday party in Wollaton (sadly I can find no information about what date or year it was or even the young ladies name but I could take you straight to the house) or Easter or Christmas visits to the local hospitals with the players but sadly it never happened.

On Saturday April 14th 2007 Notts lost at home to Walsall 2:1 with Lawrie Dudfield equalising before half time it was Walsall's promotion party and during the game Adam Cliff who was a Junior Magpie with Daniel but who was now at university approached me and asked me if he could do an interview with me as part of his dissertation for his degree regarding Notts County's record breaking 534 days in administration and the fear that the home game against Luton on Saturday September 3rd 2003 could have been their last ever game as at the time they were due to be wound up 6 days later! That day supporters from all over the country and even some from abroad came to offer their support to the club. I happily agreed so a few hours later I found myself at home being interviewed about me my life and my love of Notts County! If you really want to see a part of his work it is on You Tube under the heading Notts County "Who Ate All The Pies".

On Saturday 8th May 2010 Notts travelled to Torquay for the last game of the season and a promotion party as they had already won the league! Loraine Dan and Kim went sadly I couldn't get the time off work so had to stay behind but luckily I didn't miss all the fun! On the Sunday afternoon there was a civic reception for the club at the council house and as Loraine was still working at the club at the time she was able to get us all inside the council house and I was able to lift and hold the League Two trophy Notts had won.

On Tuesday August 3rd 2010 it was Loraine and mines 25th wedding anniversary and my last appearance as Mrs Magpie at a charity event. 27 mascots took part in the first ever Daffodil Derby, raising funds for Marie Curie cancer care. The race was due to be started by Tim Lovejoy at 7:45pm and the winner would win a day for two with the Red Arrows. I had one burning ambition left (sadly) to come last in a race as I had no chance of winning. Kimberley was Mr Magpie so that created the first problem with the greatest of respect she had as much chance of winning as I did. I spoke to a few other mascots especially Deepdale Duck from Preston who had an uncanny knack of always finishing last and it was agreed that I could finish last which I duly did. The race was won by Rammie (Derby County) running the furlong in 27.9 seconds not bad I must admit with H'Angus (Hartlepools) second and Lucas the Kop Cat (Leeds United) third. Unfortunately Mr and Mrs Pavis were not exactly impressed with the Magpies performance as Mr Magpie came 26th and Mrs Magpie 27th. Sadly soon after the race at Southwell my marriage broke down. I was totally to blame but with Loraine working at the club I thought it was the right thing to do to relinquish my post as Mrs Magpie and disappear off the scene! It was one of the hardest decisions I have ever had to make. I loved my time as Mrs Magpie and felt a part of me would always "be her". I did my duty as

Mrs Magpie for the first three home league games of the 2010/11 season, my final appearance being a 4:0 win over Yeovil on Saturday September 4th. Craig Westcarr and 2 from Ben Davies putting us three up by half time Lee Hughes getting the fourth in the second half not a bad way to sign off.

Over the years I must have been Mrs Magpie at over 200 home league games as well as 70 or 80 away ones. I loved every minute of it and there isn't a Saturday goes by in the football season when I don't wish I was still out there entertaining the crowd. During my years as Mrs Magpie I have had many husbands from Sheena Hawkridge to Tony Cotterill, Mik Wyer to Neil Mason, my 1st wife Loraine once, my daughter Kimberley a few times, my son Daniel once, Gary Seagrave Gary Ratcliffe and Kevin Humphrey the majority of them did it for the same reason, as me the love of a great football club, but sadly one or two of them did it solely for a free ticket to home games and never had any intention of going to away games or mascot events but I would like to thank all of them. It was great fun certainly for me and if circumstances were different, I am sure even at my age, I would still be prancing around. In my time, I reckon I was mascot either during mascot events or during games at roughly 45 grounds from Bolton to Bradford QPR TO Brentford, Collingham to AFC Telford United Southport to Southend and at every ground I visited I went through the same ritual, I scored a goal at both ends, so I estimate not counting the goals at Meadow Lane, that I have scored about 90 goals for Notts County. Add to that the ones at home and it must put me clear of Mr Bradd! Putting Mrs Magpie high up in the ranks of leading scorers not bad for an old bird with two left feet. As mascot I tried my best to interact with the players which wasn't always easy but I regularly had a laugh and a joke with Richard Liburd, and Gary Owers was fabulous, a great bloke. Thank you Notts County and from the Supporters Club Iris Smith for giving me the opportunity to be Mrs Magpie for so many seasons! As I have already said I loved every minute. I was in costume in fair weather or foul and was so proud to represent my club at grounds and mascot events throughout the country.

Last year at Worcester Royal Grammar School Me bottom row on right.

My children Daniel and Kimberley.

My wife Loraine, Daniel and Kimberley,
Wembley Stadium dressing room.

Mr and Mrs Magpie in the tunnel at Meadow Lane. Me on the Left.

Mr and Mrs Magpie at Huntingdon for the Mascot Grand National.

24 hour Football Marathon me front row right.

Me with the Nottingham Forest mascots head.

Me as Mrs Magpie.

Me Mrs Magpie (on the floor at the front) at Rockingham.

Lightning Source UK Ltd.
Milton Keynes UK
UKHW020316271018
331301UK00006B/115/P